Language and Literacy Series

Dorothy S. Strickland, FOUNDING EDITOR
Donna E. Alvermann and Celia Genishi, SERIES EDITORS

ADVISORY BOARD: Richard Allington, Kathryn Au, Bernice Cullinan,
Colette Daiute, Anne Haas Dyson, Carole Edelsky, Janet Emig,
Shirley Brice Heath, Connie Juel, Susan Lytle, Timothy Shanahan

---

Volumes in the NCRLL Collection: Approaches to Language and Literacy Research

JoBeth Allen and Donna E. Alvermann, EDITORS

*On Critically Conscious Research:
Approaches to Language and Literacy Research*
Arlette Ingram Willis, Mary Montavon, Helena Hall,
Catherine Hunter, LaTanya Burke, and Ana Herrera

*On Ethnography:
Approaches to Language and Literacy Research*
Shirley Brice Heath and Brian V. Street,
with Molly Mills

*On Formative and Design Experiments:
Approaches to Language and Literacy Research*
David Reinking and Barbara A. Bradley

*On the Case:
Approaches to Language and Literacy Research*
Anne Haas Dyson and Celia Genishi

*On Qualitative Inquiry:
Approaches to Language and Literacy Research*
George Kamberelis and Greg Dimitriadis

ON
CRITICALLY CONSCIOUS
RESEARCH

Approaches to Language and Literacy Research

(An NCRLL Volume)

Arlette Ingram Willis
Mary Montavon
Helena Hall
Catherine Hunter
LaTanya Burke
Ana Herrera

Teachers College, Columbia University
New York and London

NCRLL
National Conference on Research
in Language and Literacy

Published by Teachers College Press, 1234 Amsterdam Avenue, New York, NY, 10027

Published in association with the National Conference on Research in Language and Literacy (NCRLL). For more about NCRLL, see *www.ncrll.org*

Library of Congress Cataloging-in-Publication Data

   On critically conscious research : approaches to language and literacy research / Arlette Ingram Willis . . . [et al.].
        p. cm. — (Language and literacy series (NCRLL set))
   Includes bibliographical references and index.
   ISBN 978-0-8077-4906-7 (pbk. : alk. paper).
   ISBN 978-0-8077-4907-4 (hardcover : alk. paper)
   1. Education Research—Social aspects—United States. 2. Language arts—Research—Social Aspects—United States. 3. Elite (Social Sciences)—United States. 4. Critical theory. I. Willis, Arlette Ingram.
   LB1028.25.U6053 2008
   370.720973—dc22   2008017460

ISBN 978-0-8077-4906-7 (paper)
ISBN 978-0-8077-4907-4 (hardcover)

Printed on acid-free paper
Manufactured in the United States of America

15   14   13   12   11   10   09   08   8   7   6   5   4   3   2   1

Contents

From the NCRLL Editors

Research is a power play. Issues of power, too often unexamined, underlie most if not all studies. Compounding unequal relationships among researcher and researched are oppressive historical, societal, and interpersonal inequities at multiple intersections of race and religion, gender and ethnicity, sexual orientation and social class—to name only a few. *On Critically Conscious Research* by Arlette Ingram Willis, Helena Hall, Mary Montovan, Catherine Hunter, LaTanya Burke, and Ana Herrera not only asks researchers to consider these issues of power—to develop a critical consciousness—they also provide historical and contemporary tools for doing so. This provocative, scholarly volume will challenge your thinking, expose unexamined assumptions, and perhaps even upset your equilibrium. That's exactly what the authors intend, and they make their case powerfully. The authors will inspire you to design, conduct, and interpret research in critically conscious ways.

Beginning with the authors' overview of a history of ideas in critical theorizing, the reader travels in time and space through Europe as well as North and South America in an examination of critical theory. As the authors explore our roots as critical language and literacy researchers, they emphasize the contributions of African American, feminist, and Latin American scholars and social activists who have often been ignored by Eurocentric researchers. Grounded in this expanded history, readers are then invited to consider critical approaches to qualitative research in general and discourse analysis, ethnography, and policy analysis specifically. The authors apply an interlocking model posed by Patricia Hill Collins (1990, 2000) to analyze key critical studies in language and literacy. Given the history and continuing impact of educational inequity, this analysis has strong political relevance to us as educational researchers.

We believe that this book, like others in the NCRLL collection, will be useful to a wide range of researchers: graduate students, novice researchers, and experienced researchers who want to learn about an unfamiliar research tradition or methodology. Further, this volume will be valuable to researchers in other traditions who seek to develop a critical consciousness.

On Critically Conscious Research is the fifth volume in the National Conference on Research in Language and Literacy (NCRLL) collection of books published by Teachers College Press. These volumes, written by some of the most prominent researchers in the field, offer insights, information, and guidance in understanding and employing various approaches to researching language and literacy. The NCRLL organization arranges peer reviews of all titles in the series, and we'd like to thank our reviewers, including Carol Lee and Ernest Morrell, for their insightful readings of early drafts of this volume.

The first four highly acclaimed books in the NCRLL collection are *On Qualitative Inquiry* by George Kamberelis and Greg Dimitriadis, *On the Case* by Anne Haas Dyson and Celia Genishi, *On Formative and Design Experiments* by David Reinking and Barbara Bradley, and *On Ethnography* by Shirley Brice Heath and Brian Street with Molly Mills. Subsequent books in this collection will include explorations of discourse analysis in classrooms by David Bloome, Stephanie Power Carter, Beth Morton Christian, Samara Madrid, Sheila Otto, Nora Shuart-Faris, and Mandy Smith; teacher inquiry by Dixie Goswami, Ceci Lewis, Marty Rutherford, and Diane Waff; narrative inquiry by David Schaafsma and Ruth Vinz; mixed methods by Robert Calfee and Melanie Sperling; and quantitative research methods by P. David Pearson and Barbara Taylor.

The "On . . ." books: where language and literacy researchers turn to learn. Welcome to the conversation.

—JoBeth Allen & Donna E. Alvermann,
NCRLL Editors

Acknowledgments

When approached by the NCRLL series editors several years ago about writing a book that focused on critical theory and language and literacy research, I realized it was not a task that I could accomplish by myself. The journey of this text began with my group of outstanding graduate students. Together we have learned a great deal about Critical Theory and critical theories: their history, evolving status, application in language and literacy research, as well as our individual and collective commitment to equity and social change. I am most grateful to the series editors and my graduate students for this opportunity.

Collectively, we thank the NCRLL series editors (JoBeth Allen and Donna Alvermann) and the early reviewers for their careful and thoughtful support. We also extend our appreciation to the editors at Teachers College Press who have patiently worked with us to bring this project to fruition.

Arlette Ingram Willis. I thank my Lord and Savior Jesus Christ, from whom all blessings flow. With deep appreciation to my parents, Angie White Ingram and the late Adell Ingram Sr., who instilled within me a sense of social justice—informed by their belief in Christ and His power—to make a way where there appears to be no way; I am and will remain, eternally grateful. I also thank my sons, Lenny, Justin, and Jacob, whose lives serve as an inspiration for my work. Finally, I thank my husband, Leonard, who has been a constant support of my activism, advocacy, and research.

Mary Montavon. To the teacher and student in all of us, that we remain focused and steadfast in our critique of those educational institutions and their agents who extinguish the spirit of our young. Especially to my husband of 35 years, Jack, my *chroidhe dhil*, and my children, Andrea, Mary Elizabeth, and John, who enliven my spirit.

Catherine Hunter. I thank God, who created heaven and Earth, for giving me two profoundly wise and gracious parents, Homer and Lucille Hunter. I thank them for their love, guidance, and the countless sacrifices they made to give me the quality of life and education that has positioned me to participate in this powerful project. I also thank my sisters and brothers for their encouragement, unwavering love, and support. I am deeply grateful to Dr. Violet J. Harris, my friend and mentor, for always modeling the height, breadth, and depth of excellence and integrity in scholarship and friendship. Finally, I thank my professor and advisor, Dr. A. I. Willis, for welcoming me into this community of emerging scholars and shepherding our efforts, inquiry, and insights through many drafts to this completed work. Thanks so much for this opportunity and experience.

Helena Hall. I wish to thank my parents who have supported me during my educational endeavors.

LaTanya (Burke) Lambert. Many thanks to Dr. Arlette I. Willis for her perseverance in this project and for including our graduate work alongside her research studies. I want to acknowledge my time spent at the University of Illinois at Urbana-Champaign for exposing my mind to ideas about literacy and pedagogy where race and culture are concerned. My training and development as an educator were very much shaped by the relationships I was able to build with the prolific women whose names appear on the cover of this publication, and I want to show gratitude for that connection. Ladies, our coming together for this project was not coincidental but a destined opportunity, and I want to acknowledge that sense of favor and destiny in our lives and futures.

Ana Herrera. Thank you to Professor Willis, who taught me the strength and depth of cultural capital. Without the leadership and profound commitment of teachers like Professor Willis, my effectiveness and potential for fostering empowerment in my community would be dwarfed. As a result of this work, I am an agent of change, and for that opportunity—to serve children—I am eternally grateful.

To those who struggle daily and who make moment-by-moment sacrifices, to those who advocate for the oppressed, and to those who have died in the fight for equity, we stand in solidarity. With deep and sincere appreciation to all critically conscious laborers, whose unselfish devotion to equity and social justice has made this project possible, we revere and honor you.

Introduction

In this book we focus on how critical theory/ies are manifested in language and literacy research. Because this is an introductory text, we have put aside our individual interests and disengaged from complex and meaty conversations and debates in the field to focus more closely on what we believe are the most important ideas, concepts, and challenges of critical theorizing. Where does one draw a line in the sand among ideas, if at all? Disentangling ideas, especially ideas that are intimately linked to how critical approaches are envisioned, has been both daunting and inspirational. Clearly, multiple ideas are part of a broad conversation surrounding the evolution of critical theory/ies and the nexus of critical theory/ies, language, literacy, and pedagogy. However, there are ideas that have not been, but should be, part of critical theorizing and application—ideas that can inform and extend the way critical approaches are understood, applied, and adapted. We acknowledge that there are many people who have been on the front lines fighting against injustice whose scholarship and activism is not, and cannot, be named. On these ideas and on their shoulders, we stand and write.

There is no singular critical history, theory, method, methodology, or praxis. We place the notion of critical theorizing within a larger history of ideas—where critical consciousness is unbound by time and geography. From this position, it is possible to discuss critical consciousnesses in various places in the world, at various times in history, and at varying levels in language and literacy research. Using a broad notion of critical consciousness also allows us to acknowledge some overlooked roots and routes to the present as we predict how branches of theorizing may emerge and transform language and literacy research in a democratic society to become more equitable. To ensure that this book has contemporary relevance, we have tried to balance the historical grounding with current critical language and literacy research.

We present an overview of criticality that includes a discussion of the roots and routes of critical consciousness in Europe and the Americas, evolving definitions and applications to education, and key concepts that link variants of critical theorizing to language and literacy research. We draw upon both primary and secondary sources to read and interpret the works of early philosophers, and to support, challenge, or extend interpretations and understandings. Our aim is to present, as clearly as possible, a complex history of ideas that underpins critical consciousness and affects understandings of critical language and literacy research. This body of research reveals how ideological, hegemonic, and contextual forces inhibit or oppress language and literacy acquisition, use, and opportunities for emancipation/liberation,democracy, and freedom.

We introduce theories, concepts, and applications of critical theorizing applied to language and literacy research, including a discussion of the epistemological foundations of and approaches to critical methodology and methods. Our review and critique includes scholarship where scholars voice critical positions and where critical techniques are demonstrated. This decision to include scholarship that is not identified as critical research, though somewhat controversial, supports researchers who do not make an explicit acknowledgment of their use of critical theories, pedagogy, or recommendations, but whose research reflects critical schools of thought and interrogates the complexities of gender, class, race/ethnicity, language, immigrant status, sexual orientation, and power relations. There may be critical language and literacy researchers who are committed to the ideas of freedom, social justice, and democracy whom we may have missed; the failing is ours, not theirs.

We believe that, in an introductory text, it is imperative to present the big ideas that anchor concepts and that are foundational to understanding critical theories. Currently, critically conscious research represents multiple, intersecting, and interdisciplinary theories, methods, methodologies, and pedagogies. The research reflects forms of critical theorizing about gender and race/ethnicity. With these ideas in mind, our overview connects historical debates and controversies with current language and literacy theory and research. We believe that critically conscious language and literacy research should include multiple perspectives and should advocate for social justice.

This book reflects our understandings of critical consciousness, informed by theoretical/conceptual sources and ways of knowing as women whose lives reflect the intersections of race/ethnicity, gender, class, religion, and language oppression within domains of power. Trends in critical language and literacy research include freedom, democracy, emancipation/liberation, and social justice. We explore how language and literacy researchers have applied critical theory/ies using the matrix of domination model posed by Patricia Hill Collins (1990, 2000). Her model interrogates the intersectionality of oppression and levels of domination. The connections are myriad, certainly more than can sufficiently be covered in one book. We do, however, offer a vision for the future use of critical theorizing that envisages possibilities for social change, expresses hope in those possibilities to bring about the restoration of humanity, and makes plans for a more just and democratic world.

CHAPTER OVERVIEW

The first chapter presents critical consciousness as part of a global history of ideas. We offer a condensed historical overview of critical theorizing in Western Europe and the Americas, anchored by a close reading of primary sources and extended by secondary sources that interrogate criticality in general and its application in language and literacy theorizing specifically.

We begin in Western Europe with a brief discussion of the "roots" of critical consciousness by examining Critical Theory (CT), typically presented in the theories of Kant, Hegel, and Marx. We also include a discussion of The Institute for Social Research (the Frankfurt School) and the generations of activists and scholars that followed: Gramsci, Fanon, and French social theorists. In Chapter 2, our discussion extends to a focus on the contributions of African American scholars and social activists and like-minded Whites in their quest to address oppression in the United States. Our focus on African American scholars and social activists helps counter notions of critical consciousness as being primarily rooted in Western-Eurocentric thinking. Our more global examination of critical consciousness also extends to Latin America in our overview of the work and influence of Paulo Freire. We offer a snapshot of his work, focusing on critical theorizing, critical literacy, and language pedagogy. We also include Stuart Hall's writing on theory and pedagogy because it is fundamental to approaches used in critically conscious language and literacy research.

Chapter 3 provides a brief overview of the contributions to contemporary understandings of critical consciousness by critical theorists and pedagogues in the United States. These contributions are informed by Critical Race Theory (CRT) and its progeny (LatCrit, Critical Indigenous Studies, and Critical White Studies), and critical feminisms. Chapter 4 explores critically informed methods and methodologies that are used in qualitative research, discourse analysis, ethnography, and policy analysis.

Chapters 5, 6, and 7 consist of our review and critique of critical language and literacy research from 2000 to 2005. We reviewed research drawn from *Harvard Educational Review, Journal of Literacy Research, Reading Research Quarterly, Research in the Teaching of English,* and *Teachers College Record*, as well as *Discourse, Language Arts,* and *Reading Teacher*. Inspired by the interdisciplinary nature of critical consciousness and its applications to literacy and language research, we also draw on scholarship from *Anthropology and Education* and *International Journal of Qualitative Research.*

We believe that Collins's (1990) model offers a complex, sophisticated, and appropriate approach for the review and critique of current research. Chapter 5 addresses the structural and disciplinary domains of power. Chapter 6 addresses the hegemonic domains of power, and Chapter 7 addresses the interpersonal domains of power. We critique select studies in order to demonstrate how an intersecting analysis that explicates domains of power is helpful in moving theories of criticality forward.

Our review and critique is positioned as a way to challenge hegemonic ideology and traditions in the field, to address injustice and equity, to open necessary conversations about critical theorizing, and to interrogate passive language and literacy research. We envisage critical language and literacy research that more explicitly supports democracy, emancipation, freedom, and liberation in theory and praxis. As scholars adopt and adapt criticality in their quest to "speak truth to power," they should proceed cautiously. Power has become its own truth, yet Truth is its own power.

CHAPTER 1

A Framework for Understanding Critically Conscious Language and Literacy Research

I am because we are, and we are because I am.
—Igbo proverb

Throughout history, there has been irresolvable suffering in the world, and it continues in this millennium. Where do we start counting/discounting and disentangling aggression, colonization, genocide, and imperialism? How do we account for complacency, passivity, and malaise toward histories of ideological, political, and social domination? Globally, successive generations experience a legacy of capitalism, colonialism, ethnic cleansing, mass killings, oppression, slavery, terrorism, and war. As global and national challenges overlap, an awakening of critical consciousness is needed to address human suffering. Our national landscape, for example, is fraught with examples of injustice, forming mental pictures that we carry with us, from the delayed response to the needs of U.S. citizens in the aftermath of Hurricanes Katrina and Rita in 2005, to the political impasse on the immigration status of nonresidents, to the incarceration of uncharged U.S. citizens in jails and prisons. These and other mental pictures, examples, and stories of injustice—global, national, local, and personal—are experienced on a level and felt in a space so unfathomable that it almost defies words in any known language, so excruciatingly painful and so inscrutable that words nearly fail to capture the complexity of human responses.

What compelling evidence can be offered to move someone to respond with love, compassion, respect, and support to end another human's suffering? We believe that readers might develop an emotional or empathetic response to a moving story, or experience a shift in empathy; however, these responses are not synonymous with adopting a critical consciousness. Developing a critical consciousness begins long before a story is read or told as part of ongoing lifelong processes and responses to injustice—reminiscent of the critical project—drawing attention to the struggle for emancipation, liberation, and democracy. We submit that human suffering is universal, in the sense that it is not limited by geography, politics, or social constructions/categories of race, class, gender, sexual orientation, religion, and so forth. We also submit that human suffering is particularistic, in the sense that it is individual and collective, seamless and obvious, and sustained and resisted. There is no hierarchy of human suffering and no story or set of experiences so awe-inspiring as to move someone who is not predisposed to embrace critical consciousness to do so.

How did we reach this conclusion? This book evolved out of a graduate course taught several years ago where we came together as a diverse group of female scholars—women of Color and White women; immigrants and U.S. citizens; women of varying ages, socio-economic classes, and academic achievement; and women who are multi-lingual, mono-lingual, and multi-cultural. We came together to better understand criticality, especially as used in language and literacy research. We began by reading notions of Critical Theory (CT; capitalized as part of the traditional notion informed by the thinking of Kant, Hegel, Marx, and generations of the Frankfurt School) in primary and secondary sources. We often felt that some groups as well as individuals and their experiences of alienation, domination, oppression, and power were unaddressed.

Our realizations served as an epiphany that freed us to aggressively consider the underlying tensions within critical theorizing. From a historical perspective, early theorizing ignored and marginalized the critical consciousnesses of people of Color and women, and when it did mention them, it perpetuated stereotypical and deficit ideas. We found that histories of CT and some contemporary descriptions of CT, for example, place White women's oppression on the periphery and delimit the oppression of women of Color under White women's. We believe that singular, narrow, and bounded notions fail to explain the intersectionality of various forms of oppression. This interpretation points to fissures within criticality that contest attempts at universalism.

There are two competing themes in much of the language and literacy research that embraces criticality. First, some researchers do not seek to understand the intersections of class, race/ethnicity, gender, and sexual orientation, and so on, and others aim to resurrect class as a central theme of critical theorizing. Second, there is increasing pressure in the field to move understandings of criticality beyond the local to the global and to ensure universality of criticality.

Critically conscious researchers can draw from a wide range of philosophical thought to inform their work. Many envision their work as being multiperspective—a stance informed by multiple philosophical and ideological perspectives that are adopted and adapted to address emancipation, liberation, social justice, and democracy. Although this position is often used to underwrite critical theorizing, a multiperspective positioning is not synonymous with CT or critical theories (lowercase to reflect expanded notions of criticality that directly and expressly address race, class, gender, sexual orientation, religion, and their intersectionality). Our response to the diversity within critical projects has been to write a book that embraces both CT and critical theories, framed as critical consciousness.

The collective thinking of numerous theorists and advocates forms the bedrock for today's critical theorizing and research. Any discussion of criticality without an understanding of its historical and social foundations is fantasy. Generally, discussions of critical theory begin by asking the question "What is critical theory?" and then proceed to answer by explaining what critical theory is *not*. We submit that understanding critical consciousness is foundational to understanding critical theorizing. We prefer to acknowledge that there are multiple and shifting definitions of *critical theory* and expanding applications. To that end, throughout this book, we also seek to broaden the idea of critical consciousness by de-Anglicizing its histories and legacies before addressing its place in language and literacy research.

From a historical and theoretical perspective, we suggest that at the heart of critical theorizing is critical consciousness. It is this idea of critical consciousness that permeates this book. Discussions of critical theory often start with an examination of the evolution of consciousness in Western European philosophy because it is foundational to understanding how the field has been shaped, its current debates, and its ongoing controversies. However, we acknowledge that critical consciousness is not bound by time or geography, but by our own lack of understanding of non-Western philosophical thought. The importance of these moorings should not be taken lightly because they must precede discussions of critical theorizing in language and literacy research. A series of four related questions guides our overview of critical theorizing and our review and critique of language and literacy research:

> What are the epistemological roots and routes of critical
> consciousness?
> What does critical consciousness look like when applied to
> education?
> How does a critically conscious perspective impact methods and
> methodologies?
> How has critically conscious research been applied in language
> and literacy research?

Given space limitations, it is not possible to offer an in-depth overview of critical theory, so we have taken a short cut by adopting what we call the "long view." Specifically, we offer a summative review of the thinking of key figures (Kant, Hegel, and Marx) on the fundamental issues and recurring themes of critical consciousness, while acknowledging that there are other scholars (Socrates, Plato, Aristotle, Bacon, Descartes, Locke, and Hume, among others) who are not mentioned. What follows in a collapsed sense of history is a representative sampling of the evolving idea of consciousness in the West that is accessible in the works of Kant, Hegel, Marx, and later generations of critical scholars and activists who should not be read as the totality of their thinking or concerns. Then, we introduce, trace, and document the thinking of these scholars in relation to long-standing, unresolved criticisms of CT regarding issues of race/ethnicity and gender, which have become fissures in the field. Next, we highlight current positions in CT on race/ethnicity and gender. Finally, we describe the model we have adopted and adapted to discuss critical language and literacy research in an overview of the book's chapters.

CRITICAL CONSCIOUSNESS

Philosophy centers on understanding consciousness or the state of awareness of one's internal world (including emotions) and external world (including the environment). An individual's consciousness is always evolving, changing, and refining itself. In this sense, there is not one state of consciousness, but multiple interlaced consciousnesses that form a matrix of understandings influenced by the contexts of our internal and external worlds. What makes a person critically conscious is challenging the underlying assumptions that work in the internal and external worlds to privilege some while disprivileging others. We offer a sociohistoric window into Western-Eurocentric consciousness because it permits an examination of the evolution of criticality. To do otherwise is antithetical to critical theorizing. Ideas expressed by Kant, Hegel, and Marx are situated within contexts (historical, political, social, and cultural) as each scholar drew upon, extended, refined, and, in some cases, reframed the work of his predecessors. Wiggershaus (2006) suggests that, initially, CT was philosophically more holistic than is typically understood. It included religion and empirical research in response to the circumstances of history in which the scholars lived.

Kant, for instance, proposed that consciousness is a separate thought process from metaphysics and science. His explication of consciousness included alienation, autonomy, freedom, ideology, and morality. Hegel refined Kant's idea of individual and collective consciousness to include self-consciousness as a way of validating human thought and free thinking. He built upon concepts derived from Kantian philosophy and emphasized themes such as domination, equality, emancipation/liberation, empowerment, oppression, and resistance. Further, Hegel's thinking was informed by Johann Fritchie's German idealism and captured in Fritchie's triad—thesis–antithesis–synthesis, commonly referred to as the dialectical method. Hegel's application of dialectics to reality is his major contribution to CT.

Marx and Engels inverted Hegel's notion of dialectics. First, they extended consciousness by emphasizing social practice and the material world. They believed that people were socially connected through their environment, where social relations are either dependent on or independent of the material forces of production. They called the sum of such relationships the *political economy*, which forms the foundation of society. Second, they replaced Hegel's emphasis on human beings' response to their environment with an emphasis on how the environment determines human beings' consciousness.

Kant, Consciousness, and Knowledge

Kant's notion of consciousness is central to understanding CT (Hoy, 1991). He sought to establish an understanding of epistemology, separate from empirical and metaphysical thinking. He explained the importance and content of experience and its role in human knowledge: Humans can think, can have autonomous thought, and can "know" through reason. They can judge or test other thoughts through reasoning in an effort to find the truth. Kant's idea of consciousness placed knowledge and "truth" beyond the metaphysical realm, and implied that empirical or scientific knowledge was limited to the human understanding of epistemology. He believed that science was incapable of leading to an understanding of the functions of the mind and the soul. He maintained that, philosophically, our consciousness—an awareness of our thinking, our understanding, and our experience of the world—shapes knowledge. In Kant's (1965b) words, "Our knowledge springs from two fundamental sources of the mind; the first is the capacity of receiving representations . . . the second is the power of knowing an object through these representations" (p. 75). His notions of knowledge of self imply that humans can be conscious of their thinking, their world, and their experiences in the world; that self-knowledge will lead to an improved understanding of how to function in the world; and that there is also a link between understanding and reasoning. Part of Kant's appeal, then as now, was his ability to succinctly capture and articulate the importance of everyday events (Bronner, 2002). Kantian philosophers suggest that his theorizing has universal appeal. Others view Kant's thinking as explicitly racist and sexist because he invoked a racial and gendered hierarchy to explain which people are human, moral, and rational.

Hegel, Consciousness, and Knowledge

Hegel's (1977) work is understood as a critique of Kant. Three key ideas emerge from his thinking: (1) The individual is part of the culture in which s/he lives, and notions of selfhood evolve from experiences; (2) philosophy's goal should be to understand how this occurs in humanity; and (3) there are connections between reason and history. Hegel envisaged an evolutionary process of consciousness consisting of sense-certainty, perception, understanding, self-consciousness, unhappy consciousness, reason (nature, law, community), ethics, religion, and Absolute Knowing. His goal for humankind was to reach a spiritual consciousness that he believed only comes from understanding consciousness as it exists beyond self-consciousness.

The Absolute Spirit, God, is the embodiment of the finest level of consciousness. Hegel believed that true consciousness looked outward to the social world and assumed social responsibility, especially within one's locality. He believed that one of the major problems facing the modern world is the feeling of isolation or alienation. Hegel understood alienation as a contradiction of freedom and believed that historical progress hinged on finding a resolution to alienation. He created the Master/Slave relationship as an example of coming to consciousness and desiring freedom.

Marx, Consciousness, and Knowledge

The thinking of Kant and Hegel influenced Marx, who sought to discover the laws by which a society changes over time; he called his theory "historical materialism." Marx and Engels (1980) laid out their ideas of historical materialism, claiming, "Consciousness can never be anything else than conscious existence, and the existence of men is their actual life-process" (p. 14). They portend that consciousness could not make human beings independent: "the starting-point is consciousness taken as the living individual; in the second it is the real living individuals themselves, as they are in actual life, and consciousness is considered solely as *their* consciousness" (p. 15, italics in the original). Marx and Engels also believed that consciousness is a state of mind—a mere abstraction of historical development with intrinsic value; for the individual, it is called "self-consciousness." What they sought was something more "real" that could be seen. Marx believed that consciousness, as an idea, was formed in response to social and economic contexts. He proposed an inversion of Hegel's notion of consciousness by historically tracing how consciousness was formed through social and economic relationships.

Marx supported Hegel's emphasis on the importance of social relations in forming consciousness, but felt that the concept of social consciousness was inadequate to explain changes in history. He observed that "the world" was in the stage of capitalism, where the work of the lower classes is used by the wealthy upper classes to obtain and maintain wealth. He argued that the lower classes were often exploited by the upper classes; alienated from their work, themselves, and the upper classes; did not work for their improvement; and were part of the commodity fetish. He hoped that a revolution by the lower classes would bring about social change. Marx (1977) characterized consciousness within his understanding of capitalism:

> In the social production of their existence, men inevitably enter into definite relations . . . independent of their will, namely relations of production appropriate to a given stage in the development of

their material forces of production. The totality of these relations of production constitutes the economic structure of society . . . to which correspond definite forms of social consciousness. . . . It is not the consciousness of men that determines their being, but on the contrary their social being that determines their consciousness. (p. 388)

He also maintained that it was important for societies to understand the history of this process, which he outlined in *Das Kapital* (1996). Marx believed that the history of the world could be explained as a series of economic events that helped some people increase their wealth through the labor of others, who struggle to free themselves from their oppressive conditions.

Kant, Hegel, and Marx most fully recognized consciousness and critical consciousness as residing in the minds and lives of (White) males. Present in their writings are references to women and people of Color, albeit not as oppressed people. Further, their misperceptions of consciousness and knowledge as ways of meaning-making in the lives of people of Color and women have, over time, become universalized and reframed in more inclusive, human terms.

RACE AND GENDER
IN CRITICAL THEORIZING

Kant, Hegel, and Marx reveal that they held strong notions of race and gender differences, although, with few exceptions, the biographers, historians, and researchers who have examined their contributions to CT elect to homogenize, or, in some cases, omit their views on issues of race/ethnicity and gender. On the one hand, their beliefs reflected the prevailing or popular opinions of their time. On the other hand, their beliefs reflect the personal values shaped by each man's theorizing and influenced the way they viewed tensions between the real and idealized worlds. It is imperative to examine the thinking of these scholars surrounding race/ethnicity and gender because they are flashpoints in contemporary criticality and in language and literacy research. Their thinking about race/ethnicity and gender has been a stumbling block for some researchers who are seeking to uncover how consciousness sustains persistent social injustices for others.

Race Consciousness in Kant, Hegel, and Marx

Kincheloe and McLaren (2005) posit that criticality is a tradition that is under constant change. One such change has been a rethinking of the assumption that declarations by White males are universal. For instance, Kant (1965a) declared in an oft-cited comment from his essay "Observations on the Feeling of the Beautiful and the Sublime" that:

> The Negroes of Africa have by nature no feeling that rises above the trifling. Mr. Hume challenges anyone to cite a single example in which a Negro has shown talents . . . still not a single one was ever found who presented anything great in art or science or any other praiseworthy quality. . . . So fundamental is the difference between these two races of man, and it appears to be as great in regard to mental capacities as in Color. (pp. 110–111)

Kant believed in the superiority of Whites over all other races and claimed that "Humanity exists in its greatest perfection in the white race. The yellow Indians have a smaller amount of talent. The Negroes are lower, the lowest are a part of the American peoples" (Kant, 1974, p. 60). His remarks on intellect, morality, and culture include (in Kant's language) Arabs, Negroes, American Indians, Asians, Jews, and South Sea Islanders, noted in his 1775 essay "On Different Races of Man." Several scholars (Eze, 1995; Judy, 1991; Krell, 2000) portend that Kant's treatise identified non-Whites as intellectual inferiors and used racist ideas to justify the role of the State in acts of colonialism, domination, and imperialism.

Varying interpretations of Hegel suggest that, on the one hand, his thoughts on race/ethnicity point to his attempts to create universal explanations of consciousness and knowledge, and on the other hand, his thoughts point to his racist ideas about people of Color in general and people of African descent in particular. Hegel (1956) wrote, "The peculiarly African character is difficult to comprehend, for the very reason that in reference to it, we must give up the principle which naturally accompanies all our ideas—the category of Universality" (p. 93). He believed that the Negro had not historically or intellectually evolved to consciousness and, at best, could only seek to imitate White males.

Debate over Hegel's thesis of the Master/Slave relationship has been ongoing. There are two general interpretations of this thesis: (1) It reflects a universal approach to consciousness, and is merely an analogy used in explaining the historical evolution of conscious-ness in the world; and (2) it reflects the real-life Master/Slave rela-tionship in the Haitian Revolution, and has been transformed into a "metaphor for class-struggle" (Buck-Morss, 2000, p. 850). The former holds a universalistic position whereby slaves become conscious of their masters' dependency on the slaves' labor and obedience. In this view, the slaves' understanding of reality shifts from only believing what they are told by their masters to developing a personal sense of reality based on new understandings. The latter holds that He-gel was informed about racial matters, globally, in his Master/Slave thesis (Alan, 2001; Buck-Morss, 2000; Eze, 1995; Gates, 1997; Krell, 2000; Verharen, 1997). This position accounts for his inclusion of the oppressor/oppressed ideas within the peculiar institution of chattel slavery experienced by persons of Color in the New World.

The role of race in Marxism also is varied and contested, as schol-ars are divided over interpretations of Marx's thinking. On the right, there are scholars who believe that Marx used the forced labor of people of Color as a historical example of the evils of capitalism—with an emphasis on class—whereby lower classes created wealth for the upper classes. Marx did not call his analysis racism because his focus was on the oppression of people as a free source of labor in a capitalist society:

> The discovery of gold and silver in America, the extirpation, enslave-ment, and entombment in mines of the Indigenous population of the continent, the beginnings of the conquest and plunder of In-dia, and the conversion of Africa into a preserve for the commercial hunting of black skins are all things that characterize the dawn of the era of capitalist production. (Marx, 1906, p. 915)

Selfa (2002) claims that Marx's references to racial/ethnic groups —Africans, Asians, Britons, Negroes, Indigenous peoples, Irish, and poor White workers—were used to illustrate how capitalism exploits the labor of the underclass to enrich the upper class, thereby placing greater emphasis on social class.

The center position is exemplified by the work of DuBois (1933), who explained Marxism in terms of racial oppression, especially the oppression of Black workers in the United States. The early writing of West (1988, 1993a, 1993b) sought to understand the connection among philosophy, race, and identity. In 1998, for example, he found links between Marxism and the experiences of people of African de-scent, specifically those living in the United States:

> Marxist theory is indispensable yet ultimately inadequate for grasping the complexity of racism as a historical phenomenon. . . . Marxist views tend to assume that racism has its roots in the rise of modern capitalism . . . although racist practices were shaped and appropriated by modern capitalism, racism itself predates capitalism. (np)

He reconceptualizes Marxist theory within Gramsci's broader understanding of culture and ideology. West (2004) recently has abandoned his harsh criticism of racism in Marxism, suggesting that concepts that focus too closely on race, class, gender, or heterosexuality are inadequate. Further, he seeks a dialogue that critiques U.S. imperialism at home and abroad, acknowledges that capitalist excess will not support the growing poverty within our hearts and souls, and insists that our rights as human beings be respected.

On the left, Grande (2000b), a Peruvian Indian, predominantly Quecha, argues that critical theorists have not engaged "current and historical tensions between American Indian intellectualism and Marxist . . . and, thus, unwittingly contribute to the absorption of American Indians in the democratic imaginary and the loss of American Indian distinctiveness as tribal, sovereign peoples" (p. 344). She proposes Critical Indigenous theorizing that is grounded in the intellectual traditions of Indigenous people.

Although some scholars argue that the notion of race as a biological determiner of intellect, morality, and beauty is passé, others recognize that race—whether construed as biological or social—is a reality that exists locally and globally.

Gender Consciousness in Kant, Hegel, and Marx

Schott (1997) believes that Kant's writing on issues of gender is contentious, acknowledging that his characterization of women is contextually situated and unflattering by today's standards. Debates rage over whether his thinking was misogynistic or was actually the beginning of feminism. Some believe that Kant's writing reflects a respect for the equality of humanity that includes women, while others argue that his works clearly point to his sexist beliefs.

It is believed that Hegel had access to and read feminist literature. Supporters of his feminist leanings suggest that his many discussions of consciousness extend equality to (White) women. For example, Hutchings (2003) sketches Hegel's theorizing in the work of several prominent early feminists, and Stafford (1997) identifies specific connections between Hegel's thoughts on women's issues and notions of rights that are linked to feminist theorizing. Hegel made clear distinctions, however, between males and females, between married and unmarried women (extending autonomy only to the unmarried), and between the allegedly superior intellectual capabilities of (White) males and what he understood as the role of (White) women within the family and society.

Marx approached the role of gender by acknowledging that women were workers within the family. He maintained that women contribute to the production and reproduction of society and family as sources of labor and the unpaid sources of domestic labor. Women's roles as producers within society are limited to sexuality and familial interests. Marx did not address the power inequalities or oppression that exists between men and women (Nicholson, 1986), nor did he consider differences among the social status of women or cultural contexts. Despite these challenges, some feminists embrace aspects of Marxism because it addresses class inequalities, in what Sydie (1987) calls the "unhappy marriage" (p. 89) of Marxism and feminism. Marxist feminists have suggested renaming reproduction to be less sexually connected and re-aligning the role of women with that of all workers. By contrast, there are feminists who believe that Marx's view presents an inadequate and incomplete view of women's contributions to society.

The unresolved concerns about race/ethnicity and gender held by the aforementioned 18th- and 19th-century scholars paradoxically foreshadows the emergence of 20th- and 21st-century gender and racial/ethnic critical theorizing. Currently, critical theorizing in the academy includes the consciousness and knowledge processes of people of Color and women from emic perspectives. This evolution marks two important shifts in critical theorizing: the appearance of racial/ethnic critical theories by people of Color and the evolution of gender studies (feminisms, masculinities, and queer) in academia. Critical language and literacy researchers can draw upon this broad range of critical theorizing in their scholarship and activism.

In sum, Kant and Hegel theorized a connection among consciousness, race/ethnicity, and gender that perpetuated the idea of an inferior status of people of Color and women, and thereby supported colonialism and imperialism. Marx's thinking on race and gender reflects his focus on economics and capitalism. Current critical theorizing seeks to more openly address race/ethnicity and gender, moving oppression and its intersection with class from the margins to the center of criticality. Moreover, other forms of oppression—including immigration status, language, sexual orientation, and religion—are addressed in current theorizing.

Conceptual Framework

We believe that critical theorizing in language and literacy research must acknowledge its historical antecedents, recognize the fissures within critical theorizing, and appreciate the importance of culture and politics on language and literacy research and praxis. Language and literacy researchers who are critically conscious challenge barriers to social change, inequality, and democracy as they resist the reproduction of the ideas and values of privileged and dominant groups. Language and literacy theorizing are particularly well suited for examining critically conscious research efforts that seek to address and resist alienation, domination, and oppression. Just as we have mental pictures, examples, and stories of injustice and human suffering in the world, many of us also carry notions about the untapped potential of critical language and literacy research to encourage equality and advocate for social justice. We challenge the status quo in language and literacy research that ignores and marginalizes oppression as we advocate for valuing, respecting, appreciating, and validating the systems of meaning-making and communicating used by all people.

The cornerstone of our review and critique of critically conscious language and literacy research brings together histories of critical theorizing and contemporary scholarship. Our view is informed by Collins's (1990, 2000) position that consciousness is "continually evolving and negotiated" (p. 285). We draw upon the *matrix of domination* concept that she defines as "the overall organization of hierarchical power relations for any society" (p. 299). Collins removes the idealized categories of singularity that often surround understandings of oppression by placing all oppression within a systematic web of relationships and connections. Further, her thinking does not place oppression on a hierarchy: "Within this model, there are no absolute oppressors or victims. Instead, historically constructed categories create intersecting and crosscutting group histories that provide changing patterns of group participation in domination and resistance to it" (Collins, 2000, p. 248).

Within the matrix of domination, there is "(1) a particular arrangement of intersecting systems of oppression, e.g., race, social class, gender, sexuality, citizenship status, ethnicity, and age; and

(2) a particular organization of its domains of power; e.g., structural, disciplinary, hegemonic, and interpersonal" (p. 299). We seek to understand how oppression is expressed in language and literacy research, and how researchers address the intersectionality of recognized systems of oppression (race/ethnicity, class, gender, and sexual orientation) as well as less recognized forms (language and immigrant status). The singularity of the aforementioned categories as identity markers is recast by Collins (2000) as systems of oppression that intersect and need to be interrogated and understood within four domains of power: (1) structural (an organization's laws, policies, and practices), (2) disciplinary (rules/bureaucracies), (3) hegemonic (ideas and ideologies), and (4) interpersonal (lived experiences of discrimination). She summarizes the domains of power this way: "the structural domain organizes oppression . . . the disciplinary domain manages it. The hegemonic domain justifies oppression, and the interpersonal domain influences everyday lived experiences and the individual consciousness that ensues" (p. 276).

Moreover, Collins (1990, 2000) indentifies three levels at work within the matrix of domination: personal biography, social and cultural, and systematic. We use her model to examine critically conscious language and literacy research published between 2000 and 2005, and to critique the field as Marcuse (1989) advocated: "critical theory is, last but not least, critical of itself and the social forces that make up its own basis" (p. 72). Our critique seeks to broaden and transform future critically conscious language and literacy research.

CHAPTER 2

A History of the Ideas Underpinning Critical Consciousness

I do not come with timeless truths.
My consciousness is not illuminated with ultimate radiances.
—Frantz Fanon, 1967, p. 7

Within the history of ideas, CT and critical theories are part of the progeny of critical consciousness. As such, they are part of humankind's response to living within changing social, political, and economic contexts. We believe it is important to acknowledge both the roots of and routes to critical consciousness, as described briefly in the Introduction to this book. For convenience, we have subdivided the roots and routes into Western European, North American, and Central American, acknowledging that geographical locations are socially constructed and temporal while ideas are fluid and unbound. The idea of roots and routes is drawn from Hall (1999), who suggests, "instead of asking what are people's roots, we ought to think about what are their *routes*, the different points by which they have come to be now; they are, in a sense, the sum of those differences." He adds, "routes hold us in places, but what they don't do is hold us in the same place. We need to . . . make sense of the connections with where we think we are *then* as compared to where we are *now*" (np).

We believe that the roots and routes to critically conscious language and literacy research are worthy of exploration. Situating our discussion this way helps us address how Fay's (1987) outline of a fully developed critical theory serves to support the status quo.

We examine key concepts derived from Marxism found in the work of generations of the Frankfurt School, as well as Gramsci, Fanon, and French sociologists. We also include North American scholarship and research from early African American scholars. We focus on the scholarship of African Americans in part to de-Anglicize notions of critical consciousness and theorizing. In addition, we discuss, albeit briefly, the work of community activists to demonstrate the knowledges produced by those who are struggling against oppression beyond the academy. Finally, we describe the scholarship of Paulo Freire and Stuart Hall, because of their popular appeal among language and literacy scholars and educators. This chapter is not a comprehensive history or review of literature, yet the ideas and concepts are important for reenvisioning critically conscious language and literacy theorizing, research, and praxis.

Western European Roots and Routes

Marxism is generally the starting reference point in Western critical social science texts. In the United States, Marxism has been portrayed as the great evil because of its opposition to capitalism; however, it is a much more complex theory. The roots of Marxism are found in the writings of Marx (1818–1883) and his close friend and supporter, Engels (1820–1895). They suggested that it is important that the world not "ignore the individuals and the world conditions which are sources of these ideas" (Arthur, 1970, p. 79). They also extended the notion of class oppression, recognizing connections among individuals, ideas, class, and power. Importantly, they maintained that an understanding of the history of social thought requires looking closely at social relationships, especially the way shifts in power are related to political, economic, and social relations. Marx equated the ownership of private property with the wealthy (bourgeois) and envisioned an economic opposite (proletariat). He placed a great deal of emphasis on history, particularly economic, political, and social history, as a way to better understand humankind's evolution in the world.

Das Insititut für Sozialforschung (Institute for Social Research)

The origins of CT can be traced to the ideas, thoughts, personalities, and writings associated with members of The Institute for Social Research, which has been called the Frankfurt School since the early 1960s (see Wiggershaus, 1994, for a comprehensive history). Numerous histories denote shifts in the Frankfurt School's emphasis between the first, second, third, and fourth generations, and also highlight changes in theoretical positioning and geographic locales. Our brief overview focuses on the Frankfurt School's initial contributions to Critical Theory.

The Frankfurt School was established in 1923 in Frankfurt, Germany, strategically between World Wars I and II. It was founded as an opportunity for the "reexamination of the very foundations of Marxist theory, with the dual hope of explaining past errors and preparing for future action" (Jay, 1996, p. 3). The scholars of the Frankfurt School variously described their work as social and theoretical materialism, critical theory of society, critical social theory, and critical theory. The CT moniker, according to Wiggershaus (1994), was used as a "camouflage label for Marxist theory" (p. 5). The initial focus of The Institute was "first and foremost to serve in the study and extension of scientific Marxism" (p. 35). Individual scholars were advocates of select Marxist principles; others preferred to focus on the writings of Kant or Hegel; and still others sought to create new theories. The founding members of the Frankfurt School—Walter Benjamin, Erich Fromm, Max Horkheimer, Leo Lowenthal, Herbert Marcuse, and Theodor Wiesengrund-Adorno—can be characterized as upper-middle- to middle-class men of Jewish descent; however, they did not embrace their Jewish or ethnic roots, preferring to place emphasis on social, cultural, and later, political issues. Other scholars who worked at The Institute included Franz Borkenau, Henryk Grossmann, Friedrich Pollack, and Karl and Rose Wittfogel, as well as doctoral students Julian Gumprez, Kurt Mandelbaum, Paul Massing, and Hilde Weiss. Wiggerhaus (1994) claims that it was Horkheimer's articulation of the participants' social and theoretical consciousness that held the group together:

> the common task was to produce a theory of society as whole, a theory of the contemporary era, whose subject would be human beings as producers of their own historical forms of life—forms of life which had, however, become alienated from them. (p. 6)

Through his vision and management, Horkheimer was able to construct a working relationship and bridge between the social-historical approach of The Institute's early years and his own interdisciplinary approach, which said that the evolution of mankind through history was driven not only by the economy but also by the social forces within society.

Horkheimer, Adorno, and Marcuse fled Germany and lived and worked in Geneva, London, and Paris before moving to the United States to avoid the Nazi takeover of Germany. While in the United States, they were far more aware of their ethnic roots, and steadfastly retained their use of German in their writing as a show of support and in the hope of returning to a more humane Germany (Jay, 1996). According to Pecora and Irr (2005), Horkheimer and Adorno moved to Los Angeles, California, in 1941, where they worked and collaborated with Acerman, Bettelheim, and Janowitz, among others, producing *Studies in Prejudice*. Other projects undertaken by members of the Frankfurt School included studies of women's attitudes toward authority in the United States, studies on the influence of unemployment on authority in the family structure, and analyses of the influence of unemployment. These activities helped reinforce CT's focus on issues of class, and also extended scholarship to race, ethnicity, and gender. As Marcuse (1968) argued:

> Critical theory's interest in the liberation of mankind binds it to certain ancient truths. . . . In maintaining that man can be more than a manipulable subject in the production process of class society . . . [critical theory] opposes not only the production of relations that gave rise to bad materialism, but every form of production that dominates man instead of being dominated by him, this idealism underlies its materialism. (p. 153)

Likewise, Bronner (2002) holds that Frankfurt School scholars re-envisioned Marxism and gave way to "a new emphasis upon 'consciousness' and the vision of a radical transformation of society. A new concern with the connection between revolutionary theory and practice made itself felt" (p. 6). He believes that the members of the Frankfurt School theorized a connection between Hegel and Marx and placed "consciousness, as well as the practical role of ideology and reification, at the forefront of theory" (p. 81). One of the greatest legacies of the Frankfurt School is its insistence that we question every institution and thought that impacts our lives. In doing so, we enhance our ability to continually discover new possibilities for social justice.

Second-Generation Critical Theorists

Second-generation Frankfurt School scholars include Oskar Neget, Claus Offe, Karl Otto-Apel, Alfred Schmidt, and Albrecht Wellmer. The most influential theorist, however, has been Jürgen

Habermas (1929–), Adorno's assistant and the philosopher who sought to renew Horkheimer's interdisciplinary approach. Habermas's scholarship has contributed to the critical project in numerous areas and global arenas. A declared Marxist for decades, Habermas seldom references his predecessors from the Frankfurt School, choosing instead to engage the ideas of Hegel, Marx, and Kant, while being critical of Marx's economic determinism. He also continues CT's evolution through reconceptualizing and redefining the critical project.

Tracing his thinking helps illustrate his shift in foci. First, in his inaugural lecture at Frankfurt University (1965), he proclaimed that "human interest in autonomy and responsibility . . . is not mere fancy. . . . What raises us out of nature is the only thing whose nature we can know: language. Through its structure, autonomy and responsibility are posited for us" (quoted in McCarthy, 1978, p. 287). Second, in his acclaimed book, *Theory of Communicative Action*, he seeks to re-create Horkeheimer's interdisciplinary approach to social theorizing and to establish a conceptual framework. Third, he posits that a new emphasis will arise as people develop more communicative action—people coming together freely and agreeing

> at the level of the nature of social subjects, knowledge that makes possible the control of natural processes turns into knowledge that makes possible the control of the social life process. In the dimension of labour as a process of production and appropriation, reflective knowledge changes into productive knowledge. (Habermas, 1987, p. 135)

Finally, focusing on rationality, he claims its importance lies in "how speaking and acting subjects acquire and use knowledge" (Habermas, 1984, p. 11). In stark contrast to the thinking of many of the first-generation scholars, especially those under whom he studied, Habermas seeks to defend and rekindle Enlightenment rationality. His project has been, in part, to expand Kant's ideas. In doing so, he has made his work both a testament to and a critique of CT. Contemporary social theorists believe that Habermas's theorizing has overcome some of the shortfalls and criticisms of CT.

BEYOND THE FRANKFURT SCHOOL

As an idea, CT also is found in the work of Antonio Gramsci (1891–1937), Frantz Fanon (1925–1961), and French sociologists.

Gramscian Influence

Gramsci, an Italian Marxist, founded the Italian Communist Party in 1921. He spoke out against oppression from his prison cell in Italy (1926–1937). While imprisoned, he wrote 34 notebooks that demonstrate his understanding and application of Marxist theory, especially as applied to political and social issues in Europe in general and in Italy specifically during the late 1920s–1930s. His *Prison Notebooks* also drew upon his personal experiences, struggles, and understandings of being oppressed, both economically and politically.

Gramsci's ideas of hegemony have distinctive Western European roots, inspired in part by Marx and Engels's (1947) position: "The ideas of the ruling class are in every epoch the ruling ideas; i.e., the class which is the ruling material force of society is at the same time its ruling intellectual force" (p. 39). Gramsci sought to distance himself from Marx's restrictive economic determinism and class struggle, and to develop a broader theory that illuminates the roles of ideology, politics, and culture in society. His critique of society, therefore, is not rooted solely in economics, and is a much more malleable tool of analysis. He believed that the ruling classes used institutions, including schools, to inculcate their ideology and to presumptively win the consent of the masses, or, in his words, "the fabrication of consent." He believed that the failure of communism was due to its focus on capitalism, centering on its control through violence and coercion. Gramsci's (1971) thoughts about hegemony shifted over time, and include intellectual, moral, and political hegemony (Forgas, 2000). *Hegemony* has come to mean any form of domination that implies power, although more modern ideas also propose that the oppressed can effect change. Hegemony is never complete; it is always shifting, changing, and adjusting to ideological and cultural struggles.

Gramsci and his followers theorize that the real struggle in society is over ideas: ideological domination, or the struggle for meaning. He observed that those who have the power to name and define ideas or reality/ies are the ruling class. A ruling class is not limited to economic status. Gramsci suggested that social transformation/ revolution was best approached through working with adversarial groups. He also held that ideological arguments would not win over power elites—they would have to be convinced through practical work or substantive change.

Frantz Fanon: A Black Response to Critical Theorizing

Frantz Fanon (1925–1961), was born to a mixed-race (African, Tamil, and White/French), lower-middle-class family on the French colony of Martinique. He was profoundly affected by the racist acts of French soldiers during their stopover in Martinique during World War II. Fanon joined the Free French Forces, was sent to France, and left the army as a decorated war hero. He returned to Martinique, completing his undergraduate degree under the tutelage of a Communist named Aimé Césaire, and studied Marx and Sartre. His work with Césaire led him to theorize that Black men were a source of labor for White men. From studying Marx, he understood class struggle, interjecting race and racism; and from reading Sartre, he learned to point to the power of language. Fanon (1967) also critiqued Kant, Hegel, and Marx for their misunderstanding of Black men's consciousness: "black consciousness is immanent in its own eyes. I am not a potentiality of something" (p. 135). He sought to humanize Black consciousness by arguing, "I am wholly what I am. I do not have to look for the universal. No probability has any place inside me. My Negro consciousness does not hold itself out as a lack. It *is*. It is its own follower" (p. 135, italics in the original).

Fanon explicitly addressed Western European colonialism and imperialism, and the oppression foisted upon the world at the hands of White men: "It is in the name of the spirit, in the name of the spirit of Western Europe, that Europe has made her encroachments, that she has justified her crimes and legitimized the slavery in which she holds four-fifths of humanity" (Fanon, 1967, p. 252). Because of European colonialism, Fanon resolutely believed that the educated citizenry needed critical consciousness to dismantle national, political, and social powers: "The search for truth in local attitudes is a collective affair. . . . The collective struggle presupposes collective responsibility at the base and collegiate responsibility at the top. . . . [E]veryone will have to compromise in the fight for the common good" (Fanon, 1967, p. 199). Fanon's contributions to critical and postcolonial theory have been criticized for their failure to include in a substantive way the concerns of Black women, as well as non-Blacks. Fanon did not aim to universalize his work, but to ensure that people of African descent were understood as fellow human beings.

Importantly, given his training, Fanon spoke about the psychic toll of oppression on the thinking of Black men, observing how power elites use language as a tool to inculcate dominant ideologies through speech and literature in the lives of the less powerful. Agreeing with this idea, Sartre (1968) wrote in the preface to Fanon's *The Wretched of the Earth*: "Not so very long ago, the earth numbered two thousand million inhabitants: five hundred million men, and one thousand five hundred million natives. The former had the Word; the others had use of it" (p. 7). Fanon's thoughts on colonialism/postcolonialism; the import of building, nurturing, and sustaining a viable critical consciousness among the oppressed; the power of language in the hands of the oppressor; and the call to activism, and even revolt, are found in the writings of subsequent critical theorists.

French Sociologists' Contributions to CT

Several French philosophers and sociologists (Althusser, Baudrillard, Bourdieu, Derrida, Foucault, and Lyotard) also have added to critical theorizing. The contributions of Bourdieu, Foucault, and Derrida in particular have influenced critical language and literacy research. Bourdieu's articulation of the notion of habitus suggests moving difference beyond social class to include culture. He saw a need, as did Fanon, to bridge the binary of objective and subjective; to understand social dynamics, including capital (cultural, social, and symbolic), as well as field, practice, and reflexivity. Foucault's thinking has informed critical theorizing, especially his framework of social history, archaeology, and genealogy. He writes that discourse, knowledge/power, and poststructuralism are important aspects of contemporary critical works on the role of hegemony and dominant ideology in society. Derrida's major contributions focus on language, deconstruction, and adopting alternative viewpoints.

THE UNITED STATES'S ROOTS AND ROUTES

We extend the roots of critical theorizing by examining some roots and routes within the United States that add balance to traditional Eurocentric viewpoints. Oppression is not limited to any particular racial/ethnic group, gender, or class; however, we center our discussion on the scholarship of African Americans while also acknowledging the scholarship and activism of others.

Roots and Routes of Oppression

The United States has a long and disturbing history of racial oppression against people of African descent. Millions of people were forced into bondage and slavery at Bance Island in Sierra Leone and taken to Gorre Island in Senegal and other African ports of departure. The power of languages and literacies to liberate thinking and to communicate beyond the use of words was recognized as laws were established and enforced that forbade people of African descent to use their knowledges, cultures, languages, literacies, and other communicative systems. To survive, slaves were forced to assimilate and acculturate in accord with their oppressors. Numerous brave Blacks and Whites defied these laws and customs, providing literacy instruction to slaves and freed Blacks. Laws that granted citizenship only to free White male landowners made it nearly impossible for people of Color to progress economically, politically, and socially.

Early on, David Walker (1830) charged Africans and their progeny to develop "a spirit of inquiry and investigation respecting our miseries and wretchedness in this *Republic land of liberty*" (p. 5, italics in the original). In an 1883 speech, Douglass (1886) used the term "the color line in America" to characterize the racial hatred that divided the nation (pp. 5–8). Autobiographically, he recalled his oppressor's reaction to his ability to read: "A nigger should know nothing but to obey his master—to do as he is told to do. . . . If you teach that nigger . . . how to read, there would be no keeping him" (p. 49). Douglass understood the importance of becoming his "own master," or developing and acting with a critical consciousness (p. 90).

Visionaries in an Inverted World: African American Scholars

African American scholars who embraced a critical consciousness include Anna Julia (Haywood) Cooper, the mother of Black Feminism; William Edward Burghardt (W.E.B.) Du Bois, a founder of the National Association for the Advancement of Colored People (NAACP); and Carter G. Woodson, the father of Negro history. Their scholarship and social activism helped supply intellectual leadership to African Americans who were seeking social transformation and justice. They defied ideological and cultural hegemony and challenged the use of science as "proof" of racial, intellectual, and moral inferiority by drawing from broader historical, cultural, and intellectual lineages as well as by highlighting political, economic, social, and racial oppression. Their lives, research, and activism foreshadow critical race theory.

Their scholarship uncovered the ideological and racist ideas that dominated Western thought and perpetuated the oppression of African Americans, which was allegedly supported by scientific facts, but more accurately affirmed social and political prejudices. Cooper (1892) exposed the hypocrisy of the feminist movement that fought for White women's rights while ignoring Black women. She also decried the rhetoric of African American men, who fought for the rights of African Americans but focused on the rights of men. In another example, Du Bois—in his classic sociological study *The Philadelphia Negro* (1899), the first case study of an African American community—situated a history of people of African descent within their lives in contemporary society. His findings revealed that the problems of African Americans were not genetic or biological, as presumed, but economic, sociological, and psychological.

Du Bois also used narratives to convey his thinking, as in *The Souls of Black Folk* (1995/1903), where he prophetically wrote, "the problem of the Twentieth century is the problem of the color line" (p. xxxi). He knew that the existence of people of African descent, prior to their enslavement, was missing in U.S. history, as was any discussion of how their enslavement in the United States shaped their consciousnesses:

> After the Egyptian and Indian, the Greek and the Roman, the Teuton and Mongolian, the Negro is a sort of seventh son, born with a veil, and gifted with second-sight in this American world—a world which yields him no true self-consciousness, but only lets him see himself through the revelation of the other world. It is a peculiar sensation, this double consciousness, this sense of always looking at one's self though the eyes of others, of measuring one's soul by the tape of a world that looks on in amused contempt and pity. One ever feels his two-ness,—an American and a Negro; two souls, two thoughts, two unreconciled strivings; two warring ideals in one dark body, whose dogged strength alone keeps it from being torn asunder. (pp. 2–3)

Du Bois's reference to the veil and second-sightedness marked the African American experience as fundamentally different from the White American experience.

Du Bois believed that to apply Marxist theories in the United States, one must consider the role of race and class oppression under capitalism. He acknowledged that the White working class in the United States stood in opposition to the furtherance of African American economic, political, and social gains. He surmised that although Marxism may be an accurate portrayal of a history of economic and social change in 19th-century Europe, it needed to be modified to address the history of economic and social change for African Americans in the United States.

Finally, Carter G. Woodson observed and commented on how the economic and social-relational forces shaped the consciousness of African Americans: "When you control a man's thinking you do not have to worry about his actions. You do not have to tell him to stand here or go yonder. He will find his 'proper place' and will stay in it. . . . His education makes it necessary" (Woodson, 1933, p. xiii). He argued that many African Americans were conscious of the efforts to coerce them into the ways of thinking, worldviews, and beliefs of Whites; many fought against coercions that questioned their intelligence, morals, and humanity. Woodson argued that what appeared to be a consensual response to the lack of education and educational opportunities by African Americans was not consent, but an illusion created by a coerced response of an oppressed people. He believed that race is central to understanding African American consciousness and life experiences in the United States:

> The same educational process which inspires and stimulates the oppressor with the thought that he is everything and has accomplished everything worthwhile, depresses and crushes at the same time the spark of genius in the Negro by making him feel that his race does not amount to much and never will measure up to the standards of others. (Woodson, 1933, p. xiii)

Woodson explained that education was shaped by ideological hegemony to neutralize pedagogical and curricular decisions—i.e., the relational forces that made possible and acceptable chattel slavery, discrimination and segregation, and physical violence (lynching, murders, mutilations, rape), and simultaneously kept, or limited, discussions of oppression enacted by the United States out of history books. He felt strongly that the U.S. system of education was structured to coerce all Americans to see African Americans as inferior to Whites, whether that inferiority was based on "science," history, or morality, and to extol the achievements of Whites. To that end, he created avenues for the publication of Negro history and books that celebrated the accomplishments of African Americans.

Collectively, these scholars demonstrated through their lives, research, and activism that the ideologies, values, and beliefs held and promoted by their oppressors must be challenged. They understood that economic oppression is insufficient to capture every form of oppression experienced by African Americans.

ALTERNATIVE U.S. ROUTES

In the mid-20th century, Black and White freedom fighters demonstrated their resistance to social injustices. Among the many fearless workers against class and racial oppression were Myles Horton (1905–1995) and liberation theologists.

Myles Horton, a White male, was the founder of the Highlander Folk School (renamed in 1961 to the Highlander Research and Education Center) in New Market, Tennessee. His life of poverty and his study of Marx and Lenin encouraged him to fight against all forms of oppression, protesting for workers' rights and participating in the civil rights movement (desegregation, voter education, and voter registration) to transform society. Horton (1998) believed that critical consciousness was necessary for social and political progress as people "learn to value their own experience, to analyze their own experience, and to know how to make decisions" (p. 57). He offered literacy programs designed to teach African Americans to read and write in order to pass literacy tests and thereby gain the right to vote.

Horton organized literacy programs by enlisting Septima Clark, a South Carolina schoolteacher and freedom fighter, who called upon her niece, Bernice Robinson, to lead the program. Robinson taught African American adults by asking them to tell her a story that she wrote down and asked them to read. She used the interests of the adults to teach them to read, and many passed the literacy tests. Horton (1998) recalled, "along with becoming literate, they learned to organize, they learned to protest, they learned to demand their rights, because they also learned that you couldn't just read and write yourself into freedom" (p. 104). Life and learning at the Highlander Folk School was unapologetically interracial. Horton declared, "to make life worth living you have to believe in those things that will bring about justice in society, and be willing to die for them" (p. 27).

Liberation theology is a form of critical consciousness based on Christian beliefs that seeks to end the suffering in the world. It identifies God's compassion for oppressed people as a starting point, unlimited by history, geography, or denomination. Believers envisage liberation theology as an expression of their faith and duty to activate Christian theology on Earth because—in an uncertain world—God is faithful. They look to Christ as Liberator (a secular label); in the Holy Bible, Christ is named Advocate, Deliverer, Good Shepherd, and Savior. Liberation theologists draw support from scriptural references to the needs of the poor (Leviticus 25:35–38; Luke 1:51–53, 4:16–18) and of the oppressed (Isaiah 61:1–2 and James 5:1–6). They carry their message to the masses through social and political activism.

The critical theological consciousness of African American Christians is without a single historical beginning point. It is informed by the works of W.E.B. DuBois, M. Garvey, F. Grimke, N. Turner, and C. G. Woodson, among others. As early as 1902, ex-slave Grimke declared, "God is not dead, nor is he an indifferent onlooker at what is going on in this world. . . . Justice may sleep, but it never dies" (quoted in Woodson, 1942, p. 354). Black Liberation Theology (BLT) evolved during the civil rights movement as the nexus of Black Power and Black Christianity, grounded in liberation theology, the Black religious experience, and the struggle for freedom. BLT embodies God's enduring and everlasting compassion, lovingkindness, trustworthiness, mercy, and grace, with a particular emphasis on spiritual and moral consciousnesses.

Proponents of BLT include James H. Cone (1938–), Benjamin E. Mays (1894–1994), Martin Luther King Jr. (1929–1968), Malcolm X (1925–1965), Adam C. Powell Sr. (1865–1953), and Adam C. Powell Jr. (1908–1972), among others. Cone (1970), a leader in the field and one of its most prolific writers, believes that White Christians, activists, and political leaders opposed the idea of dividing Christianity into a Black/White binary and promoted the idea that Christianity is universal and color-blind. Proponents of BLT argue that such universalist ideas are a continuation of a White interpretation of the Bible, a White inability to see non-Whites as human, the irreconcilable suffering of people of Color at the hands of Whites in the name of "justice," and the inculcation of dominant ideologies that impeded self-actualization among people of Color. BLT continues to address human suffering throughout the world and to promote an appreciation of African American history and culture, brotherhood, freedom, hope, liberation, love, and social justice. Moreover, BLT resists capitalism, poverty, and dominating ideologies that promote human suffering.

Garcia (1987) explains the uniqueness of liberation theology within Latindad, noting concern with "contributing to each other's work so it might be of service to the church and the formation of ministers seeking to serve our community" (p. 216). A similar activist perspective is evinced by the life and work of Paulo Freire, whose connection to liberation theology is reflected in his commitment to Catholicism and work with the World Council of Churches (he served as an educational consultant while exiled in Geneva, Switzerland). Gadotti (1994) argues that Freire's ideas fall within "a progressive conception of theology and the social and political role of the church . . . especially in Latin America and defends the involvement of Christians in the struggle for liberation" (pp. 170–171). The critical consciousness of Paulo Freire also has had a tremendous impact on language and literacy research.

PAULO FREIRE: THEORY, LITERACY, AND PEDAGOGY

Paulo Reglud Neves Freire's (1921–1997) life, scholarship, and commitment to critical consciousness and activism have been captured in numerous texts (Freire, 1995, 1996; Gadotti, 1994; A. Freire & Macedo, 1998). Freire (1996) recalled two life-changing moments that helped shape his political and pedagogical ideas. First, he observed that the economic and social conditions that caused the oppressed to fear were destructive—relational forces kept the oppressed dependent on their oppressors and dominated their bodies and every moment of their lives. He believed that oppression is economically, politically, and socially constituted. Second, as director of the Industrial Social Service (SESI), a program initially designed to educate Brazil's rural labor force, he embraced and taught the power of dialogic pedagogy. Freire recognized a gap between the education offered by the state and the education the poor needed to make informed, purposive, and proactive decisions. Further, he observed that the educational system is a key component used by power elites to retain power and status and to dominate or control the thinking of the masses through the instruction of sterile curriculums. The central idea of Freire's work, one that he believed is fundamental for social change, is *conscientização*. The concept evolved over time. For example, in 1967, he declared:

> Every relationship of domination, of exploitation, of oppression, is by nature violent, whether or not the violence is expressed by drastic means. In such a relationship, dominator and dominated alike are reduced to things—the former dehumanized by an excess of power, the latter by the lack of it. (Freire, 2002, p. 10f)

Freire identified three stages, or levels, of critical consciousness: (1) semi-intransitive consciousness (limited consciousness), (2) naive transitivity (a simple trusting attitude toward reality), and (3) critical transitivity (individual and critical awareness of problems, and the ability to engage in dialogue in search of solutions). In 1971, Freire underplayed the Marxist overtones, describing *conscientização* as

> an act of knowing, if our understanding of this act is a dialectical one. Therefore, *conscientização* cannot be either an act of transference of knowledge, nor an intellectual game, but rather—let us repeat—a real act of knowing what demands praxis. . . . [T]he process of *conscientização* which does not pass through the unveiling of reality to the practice of its transformation, is a process which becomes frustrated. (p. 4)

In 1996, Freire revealed that his focus on class was purposeful—an attempt to counter dominant ideologies. Later, he extended the concept to include "awareness of the historical, sociopolitical, economic, cultural, and subjective reality that shapes our lives, and our ability to transform that reality" (Freire, 1998, p. 340). To break the stranglehold over the minds of the oppressed, he argued that people need to become critically conscious, describing the evolution of *conscientização* as an intellectual journey. He wrote, "Being conscious . . . is a radical form of being, of being human. It pertains to beings that not only know, but know that they know" (P. Freire & Macedo, 1987, p. 127). As Gramsci and Fanon also suggested, humankind needs to develop a "critical spirit" (Freire, 2002, p. 7). Freire's ideas about consciousness, alienation, oppression, power, and resistance mirror Fanon's emphasis on the need to develop consciousness (self, critical, and collective); appreciate one's culture, the right to one's language, and the importance of education and literacy for the masses; and support social and political activism. There also are points of difference, as Fanon expressed concern about the role of dominant ideologies in misrepresenting and stereotyping the "Other," especially the cultures of the people of African descent, whereas Freire is often criticized for not addressing and opposing racism more openly.

Stuart Hall: Literacy, Articulation, and Communication

British Cultural Studies, inspired by Marxist and Gramscian thinking, surfaced in the early 1960s, in part as a response to the needs and lives of the working classes. The Birmingham School of Thought, founded by Stuart Hall, Richard Hoggart, E. P. Thompson, and Raymond Williams, evolved into the Centre for Contemporary Cultural Studies (CCCS) under the leadership of Hoggart at the University of Birmingham. The name change reflects CCCS's study of language and its effects on popular culture. During Hall's tenure as director, CCCS's focus shifted to understanding the struggle over meaning in the lives of oppressed groups. Hall, a Jamaican national, also sought to understand how racial, ethnic, and national groups make meaning, especially how they make meaning that is in opposition to mainstream representations. Hall's work focuses on how these groups struggle to re-name and re-present themselves in opposition to popular images promoted by the power elites through the media. He appreciates and accounts for the systems of knowing that both the sender and the receiver use in making meaning possible. He also envisages knowledge as multiple and complex, not singular or simplistic. Further, he provides a structure that suggests how ideological and cultural hegemonies moved from the abstract to the concrete and how they work in real time and space (Hall, 1970).

Hall's (1982) definition of *ideology* and his understanding of hegemony inform his theorizing. He defines *ideology* as "mental frameworks—the languages, the concepts, categories, imagery of thought, and the systems of representation—which different classes and social groups deploy in order to make sense of, define, figure out and render intelligible the way society works" (p. 26). He suggests that the "problem of ideology" can become a material force, where language can be used to amass or support power and domination. His ideas dismiss the call for universal approaches to knowing because he believes they ignore how knowing can only offer situated and temporal explanations at best. His notion of theoretical inadequacy punctuates how hegemony: (1) identifies traditional historical approaches and explanations of the past, and (2) explains the failure of dominant concepts, definitions, and models as explanations for the Underserved.

SUMMARY

The roots of critical theorizing extend to many geographical locales and embrace varying aspects of criticality. From the ideas espoused by Western European philosophers, sociologists, and thinkers, critical theories have emerged as a route that explicitly addresses oppression, power, and social justice. We note that the oppression of women and people of Color is not mentioned in the writings of Kant, Hegel, and Marx, as well as their successors. Unlabeled oppression, however, is nonetheless oppressive. The distinctive U.S. roots and routes of critical theorizing included in this chapter emphasize the experiences of people of Color, women, and the intersection of multiple oppressions. Our discussion of their critical theorizing, though limited, evinces the struggle for social justice, equality, and democracy.

We briefly reviewed the way Freire's notion of *conscientização* and Hall's understanding of ideology and hegemony explicate how people make meaning, how meaning-making is informed by culture and language, and how every human being has the right to communicate in ways that are culturally and linguistically authentic and appropriate.

We have considered movements within criticality and U.S. history where race and gender oppressions were marginalized as well as their current centrality. Specifically, the critical theorizing of the past, which ignored race/ethnicity and gender, found that these same forms of oppression dominate current criticality and are extended to include articulations of multiple and intersecting oppressions. More importantly, the scholarship and the voices of the oppressed are integral to new understandings of criticality.

CHAPTER 3

Critical Consciousness: Language, Literacy, and Pedagogy

Injustice anywhere is a threat to justice everywhere.
—Martin Luther King Jr., 1963, "Letter from Birmingham Jail"

U.S. social theorists (Best, 1995; Fay, 1987; Jay, 1996) posit definitions of critical theory, and Bronner (2002) identifies several key themes that frame criticality in the late 20th century: "alienation, the domination of nature, the regressive components of progress, the mutability of human nature, and the stultifying effects of the culture industry and advanced industrial society" (p. 9). He also cautions that critical theory is in a state of crisis. We consider his caution by examining the fundamental ideas that have shaped criticality in education and their connections to language and literacy research and praxis. Then, we discuss critical pedagogy and note the resurfacing debates that surround race/ethnicity and feminism.

CONTEMPORARY CRITICAL THEORIZING IN EDUCATION

There is no monolithic definition of critical theory. Kincheloe and McLaren (1994) have identified several key assumptions that inform most definitions:

> all thought is fundamentally mediated by power relations that are social and historically constituted; that facts can never be isolated from domain of values or removed from some form of ideological inscription; that the relationship between concept and object and

between signifier and signified is never stable or fixed and is often mediated by the social relations of capitalist production and consumption; that language is central to the formation of subjectivity (conscious and unconscious awareness); that certain groups in any society are privileged over others and, although the reasons for this privileging may vary widely, the oppression that characterizes contemporary societies is most forcefully reproduced when subordinates accept their social status as natural, necessary and that focusing on only one at the expense of others (e.g., class oppression versus racism) often elides the interconnections among them; and, finally, that mainstream research practices are generally, although most often unwittingly, implicated in the reproduction of systems of class, race, and gender oppression. (pp. 119–120)

Their description of criticality calls into question the dominant ideologies and hegemonic processes that are used to sustain them. Other scholars (Apple, 1982; McLaren & Giarelli, 1995; Popkewitz & Fendler, 1999) also have questioned the power relations within education and their effect on the Underserved. These scholars argue that an understanding of the notion of critical theory(ies) should include reconstructive (critical modernist) and deconstructive (postmodernist) forms. Ladson-Billings (1997), in a critique of critical theorizing, observes that it fails to "address adequately the question of race" (p. 127). She questions the use and application of CT for children of Color in education, and suggests that its use by educational researchers demands accountability. Further, she argues that race, as a social construct, has been co-opted in critical theorizing by turning to notions such as identity. Since race/ethnicity have become more central to critical theories, her critique supports a movement away from Anglocized, paternalized, and marginalized understandings of race/ethnicity and gender.

CRITICAL RACE-CONSCIOUSNESS

While the West envisages itself as transcending race/ethnicity and gender oppression, silences about past and current colonization, genocide, imperialism, and mass murders are constant reminders of human rights abuses and human suffering. Some educational researchers have embraced critical race-consciousnesses to address these philosophical and theoretical gaps in criticality.

Critical Race Theory

Critical Race Theory (CRT) emerged as a moniker for the theoretical orientation and movement among legal scholars of Color (and in response to the shortcomings of Critical Legal Scholarship). They sought to "reexamine the terms by which race and racism have been negotiated in American consciousness, and to recover and revitalize the radical tradition of race-consciousness among African Americans and other peoples of Color" (Crenshaw, Gotanda, Peller, & Thomas, 1995, p. xiv). Proponents of CRT acknowledge that the concept of race is socially constructed and is not a biological or scientific fact, while simultaneously understanding that this construct operates as "fact" within the United States. CRT is informed by Black feminist theory, critical theory, critical legal studies, feminism, liberalism, Marxism/neo-Marxism, poststructuralism, postmodernism, and neo-pragmatism. The linkages between race/ethnicity and education are found in evolving notions of Black feminism/womanism and Chicana and Mexicana feminisms (Galván, 2001). Critical theories that center on race point to the importance of race/ethnicity and the intersections of class, culture, gender, language, and immigrant status.

CRT addresses ethnicity, immigration, land sovereignty, language rights, and national origin discrimination (Lawrence, Matsuda, Delgado, & Crenshaw, 1993). According to West (1995), philosophically, CRT "puts forward novel readings of a hidden past that disclose the flagrant shortcomings of the treacherous present in light of unrealized—though not unrealizable—possibilities for human freedom and equity" (p. xii). Lawrence, Matsuda, Delgado, and Crenshaw (1993) argue that CRT helps focus on the "immediate needs of the subordinated and oppressed even as we imagine a different world and offer different values. It is work that involves both action and reflection. It is informed by active struggle and it in turn informs that struggle" (p. 3). Proponents acknowledge hegemonic forces that work against oppressed groups and reenvision the critical project on their own terms. For example, Pizarro (1998) opines that racism is an "endemic facet of life in our society and that neutrality, objectivity, colorblindness, and meritocracy are all questionable constructs" (p. 62). Collins (2000) also suggests that color-blindness is "a new rule that maintains long-standing hierarchies of race, class, and gender while appearing to provide equal treatment" (p. 279). CRT does not strive to renormalize or universalize the struggle against oppression in terms of race consciousness, but it understands the struggle as a part of a greater critique of liberalism (Delgado, 1995). Crenshaw, Gotanda, Peller, and Thomas (1995) identified two common interests in CRT:

The first is to understand how a regime of white supremacy and its subordination of people of Color have been created and maintained in America, and, in particular, to examine the relationship between that social structure and professed ideas such as "the rule of law" and "equal protection." The second is a desire not merely to understand the vexed bond between law and racial power but to *change* it. (p. xiii, italics in the original)

They also acknowledge that intersectionality or multiple forms of oppression are experienced among people of Color. CRT scholars maintain that racial categories are built on the acceptance of two fundamental untruths: (1) people can be distinguished based on phenotype (as well as physical markers), where Whites are the superior racial group; and (2) Whiteness is the norm.

Addressing Whiteness is foundational to CRT: "The real issue is not necessarily the black/white binary as much as it is the way everyone regardless of his/her declared racial and ethnic identity is positioned in relation to Whiteness" (Ladson-Billings & Donner, 2005, p. 116). The centrality of race includes the concerns of African Americans, Asian Americans, Latin Americans, and Native Americans. Ladson-Billings (2000) reviews racial discourses and ethnic epistemologies that anchor CRT, and specifically consciousness, *mestiza* consciousness, tribal secrets, heterogeneity, hybridity, and multiplicity. In addition, she discusses ethnic epistemologies among Asian Pacific Islanders, Latin Americans, and Native Americans. She argues that CRT applies not only to African Americans, but to "any people who are constructed outside the dominant paradigm" (p. 260). She observes that each group embraces ways of knowing that are not part of U.S. educational pedagogy or reform. Her point is that racial/ ethnic epistemologies are embedded in the critical consciousness of people of Color from their earliest memories, and reflect their history and culture as a people, not limited to their response to the dominant culture. Barnhardt and Kawagley (2005) add that academics need to acknowledge the consciousness of Indigenous peoples, in particular the bush consciousness of Alaska natives.

Educational researchers have adopted CRT to more adequately address the historical and present-day contexts of race, racism, and oppression. Solórzano, Ceja, and Yosso (2000) stress that CRT in education

simultaneously attempts to foreground race and racism in the research as well as challenge the traditional paradigms, methods, texts, and separate discourse on race, gender, and class by showing how these social constructs intersect to impact on communities of Color. (p. 63)

CRT continues to evolve as activists, researchers, and scholars explicitly link efforts in education and community.

Stovall (2005) applies a CRT framework in his year-long study of the Umoja Leadership Institute, where "the program itself served as a 'living text' from which to develop future ideas and projects" (p. 99). Using narratives, he "provides a 'human face' to the silenced relationship between public schools and community organizations" (p. 100). Through interviews with mentors, he identifies histories and collective efforts used to create positive change in the lives of young people. He offers a counterstory to mainstream notions of urban education that perpetuate stereotypes of academic disinterest among children of Color.

Language and literacy scholars who have adopted CRT as a lens challenge traditional theories that language and literacy are neutral, objective, and color-blind as they expose assumptions of White superiority in theories, methods, and analysis (Delgado Bernal, 1998; Duncan, 2002b, 2005). CRT reveals the importance of literacy in the lives of people of Color and the multiple consciousnesses and literacies that people of Color use. Importantly, it validates the fact that people of Color are "holders and creators of knowledge" (Delgado Bernal, 2002, p. 108). Collins (2000) identifies two types of knowledge—subjugated and oppositional—that inform understandings: (1) *subjugated knowledge* refers to the "secret knowledges generated by oppressed groups . . . hidden because revealing it weakens its purpose of assisting them in dealing with oppression" (p. 301), and (2) *oppositional knowledge* refers to "a type of knowledge developed by, for, and/or in defense of an oppressed group's interests. . . . [I]t fosters the group's self-definition and self-determination" (p. 299). CRT frameworks use narratives (autobiography, personal stories, or first-person accounts) that foreground the voice, experience, and realities that inform the consciousnesses of people of Color. Delgado Bernal (2001) believes that storytelling represents "culturally specific ways of teaching and learning that ancestors and elders [use to] share the knowledge of conquest, segregation, labor market stratification, patriarchy, homophobia, assimilation, and resistance" (p. 624). CRT challenges and critiques the use of language, literacy, and power to normalize and universalize Whiteness.

LatCrit, Critical Indigenous Theory, and Critical White Studies

LatCrit, Critical Indigenous Theory, and Critical White Studies (CWS) are additional examples of critical race-conscious theorizing that address historic and contemporary contexts, as well as legal, social, and economic issues. Two goals that anchor LatCrit scholarship, for instance, were drafted following the 1995 colloquium in Puerto Rico on Latina/o communities and critical race theory:

> (1) to develop a critical, activist and inter-disciplinary discourse on law and policy towards Latinas/os, and (2) to foster both the development of coalitional theory and practice as well as the accessibility of this knowledge to agents of social and legal transformation. LatCrit theorists aim to center Latinas/os' multiple internal diversities and to situate Latinas/os in larger inter-group frameworks, both domestically and globally, to promote social justice awareness and activism. (LatCrit: Latina & Latino Critical Legal Theory, Inc., 2007, p. 2)

The early focus of LatCrit has been legal, but it is being expanded to include a focus on social concerns, class, gender, language, immigrant status, race, and religion. LatCrit is also concerned with "a progressive sense of a coalitional Latina/o pan-ethnicity" (Solórzano & Delgado Bernal, 2001, p. 310). For example, LatCrit theory includes feminisms applied to education research by Delgado Bernal (2001, 2002), Cruz (2001), Delgado-Gaitan (1990), Elenes (2001), Galván (2001), González (2001), Hernández-Avila (1995), and Villenas (1996), among others. Delgado Bernal (2001) argues, "Chicana feminist pedagogies are partially shaped by collective experiences and community memory" (p. 624). She comments on how knowledge is shared among multiple generations of women in families to "help us survive in everyday life by providing an understanding of certain situations and explanations about why things happen under certain conditions" (pp. 624–625). Delgado Bernal adds to our understanding of biculturalism, bilingualism, and the spirituality of Chicana/os. Likewise, González (2001) acknowledges her use of *mestizaje* consciousness as "an ethical commitment to egalitarian social relations in the everyday political sphere of culture" (p. 646). Further, she draws upon *mestizaje* knowledge using a braiding metaphor where Mexicanas offer counternarratives to define themselves as active learners.

Critical Indigenous Theory. Critical American Indian and Indigenous scholars embrace the tenets of CRT and extend the epistemologies, theories, methods, and pedagogies to American Indian and Indigenous people. Guevara (2003), for instance, describes the need to change the educational system provided to Indians in South America because it does not respect their humanity. Instead, the system "filled them with shame and resentment, rendering them unable to help their fellow Indians and [putting them] at the severe disadvantage of having to fight within a hostile white society which refuses to accept them" (p. 97). Throughout his journeys, Guevara encountered Indigenous people who were being exploited for their labor and were living in substandard conditions. He marveled at their will to survive and their hope for a more just life for their progeny. Central ideas in his work include identity/authenticity, sovereign land rights, and politics.

Grande (2000b) submits that Critical American Indian Studies have been labeled a "dangerous discourse" because they challenge

> "Whitestream" advocates of critical theory to ask how their knowledge and practices may have contributed and remained blind to the continued exploitation of Indigenous peoples . . . to confront the taboo subjects of racism, sexism, and homophobia within American Indian communities. (p. 354)

She believes that American Indian epistemology must be respected and valued because it provides shadow, light, and relief to our understandings of American Indians in research projects by replacing traditional, often stereotypical, and underinformed academic perspectives and by illuminating the humanity of all people. Lomawaima and McCarty (2002) also offer a historical overview of American Indian education that includes a review of the ideological and political forces that have thwarted attempts to establish American Indian education in the United States.

McCarty, with guest coeditors Borgoiakova, Gilmore, Lomawaima, and Romero (2005), presents scholarship that highlights and questions linguistic self-determination in Indigenous communities and schools. They observe that the United Nations International Labor Organization, Convention 169 Article 1.1, states:

> *Indigenous peoples* are regarded as Indigenous on account of their descent from the populations which inhabited the country, or a geographical region to which the country belongs, at the time of . . . colonization or the establishment of present state boundaries and who, irrespective of their legal status, retain some or all of their own social, economic, cultural, and political institutions. (p. 1)

This definition is aligned with Graveline's (2000) research and should be acknowledged in critical language and literacy studies among Indigenous groups.

Critical White Studies. Central to understanding Critical White Studies (CWS) is locating race and power within the culture and politics of the United States. CWS has become a focus in the field of education (Jensen, 2005; Kincheloe, Steinberg, Rodriguez, & Chennault, 1998; Roediger, 2001), in response to the focus on critical racial/ethnic studies. Delgado and Stefancic (1997) maintain that a discussion of Whiteness is a necessary step after addressing CRT to explicate Whiteness for Whites and non-Whites. Several White scholars and critical pedagogues (Gallagher, 1995; Giroux, 1997; McIntrye, 1997; Sleeter, 1996; Weiss & Lombardo, 2003) acknowledge the pervasiveness, privilege, and authorized support of Whiteness in educational theories, teacher preparation, and instruction. Frankenberg and Mani (1993) observe:

> to speak of whiteness . . . refers to a set of locations that are historically, socially, politically and culturally produced and, moreover, are intrinsically linked to unfolding relations of domination. Naming whiteness displaces it from the unmarked, unnamed status that is itself an effect of dominance. Among the effects on white people both of race privilege and of the dominance of whiteness are their seeming normativity, their structured invisibility. (p. 6)

Ferber (2007) points out how race relations affect White people and how the exclusion of Whiteness from racial history "prevent[s] us from understanding racial privilege, relieving Whites of responsibility for racism" and continuing the tradition of privileging Whites (p. 267). Frankenberg and Mani (1993) recognize that within some discussions of Whiteness, Whites tend to see themselves as acultural or distinguish themselves by nation of origin, or ethnicity. They also argued that the "danger of whiteness coded as 'no culture' is that it leaves in place whiteness as defining a set of normative cultural practices against which all are expected to fit" (p. 204).

Language and literacy researchers Lewis, Ketter, and Fabos (2001), while working in a rural White setting, observed attitudes among White teachers and students that supported White normalcy. Weis and Lombardo (2003) found similar responsiveness among White working-class males; however, their Irish American participants sought to spend time together in an Irish center in order to resurrect their sense of Irish pride, re-instantiate cultural traditions, and debunk stereotypes. These groups were "talking uncritically with/to other Whites, all the while resisting critique and massaging each other's racist attitudes, beliefs, and actions" (McIntyre, 1997, pp. 45–46). As CWS has grown, its criticality has refocused on social class.

Michaels (2006), however, suggests that discussions of race and ethnicity have become more palatable because they challenge people to become better human beings. He sees class as a stumbling block for researchers, because there is a tacit assumption that discussions of class also call for discussions of accountability (answering questions of "why" and "how" wealth is garnered) and recognition of the power of the wealthy to maintain their wealth at the expense of the poor. Further, class discussions can imply the need to address the redistribution of wealth. Despite the current push in some critical theory camps to return to a focus on socioeconomic class, there are fears that such a return will renormalize Whiteness and re-empower Whites to categorize the oppression of people of Color within larger ideas such as globalism and internationalization while ignoring their personal, political, and collective experiences. In the lives of individuals, oppressions are not peripheral concerns; they are a threat to daily existence and survival. Duncan (2005) rebuts criticisms by Darder (2002) and Darder and Torres (2005) that suggest that race is a narrow marker that should be replaced by economic concerns.

CRITICAL FEMINISMS

We acknowledge that feminism is not a monolithic theory, but consists of multiple feminisms that engage critical consciousnesses and seek to demystify and uncover ways in which gender is used to oppress. Collectively, these feminisms address inequalities of gender, and recognize the importance of multiple ways of knowing. Weiler (1991) posits that "feminist theory . . . validates differences, challenges universal claims to truth, and seeks to create social transformation in a world of shifting and uncertain meaning" (p. 449). Critical feminisms now include notions of intersectionality that acknowledge the domains of oppression women experience. The scholarship of Brodkin (1992), Ferber (2007), and Frankenberg (1993) all addresss intersectionality in White feminisms.

Theorizing about feminisms has seen shifts from Gilligan's (1982) "feminisms of difference" to the current categorizing of feminism that includes Black, cultural, Jewish, liberal, Marxist, multicultural, postmodern, and radical, to name a few. From the Black feminist Walker (1983), who coined the term *womanism* to distinguish Black feminisms, to the groundbreaking work of Collins (1990, 1998, 2000), hooks (1984, 1994), and Dillard (2000), Black feminism/womanism continues to evolve. Collins (1990) outlined four tenets of Black feminist thought: (1) specialized epistemology, (2) dialogue to assess knowledge claims, (3) an ethic of caring, and (4) an ethic of personal accountability. Other feminist scholars of Color include explicit Latina/Chicana epistemologies and pedagogies of Anzaldúa (1990), Delgado Bernal (2001), Hernández-Avila (1995, 1997), Sandavol (2000), and Villenas (1996), as well as Allen (1986), Grande (2000a, 2000b, 2004), and Smith (1999), who speak to American Indian and Indigenous feminist perspectives.

González (2001) argues in support of a critical raced/gendered epistemology because it permits researchers to "bring together understandings of epistemologies and pedagogies to imagine how race, ethnicity, gender, class, and sexuality are braided with cultural knowledge, practices, spirituality, formal education, and the law" (p. 643). She describes her research methods as *trenzas y mestizaje*, a multimethodological approach that includes "the braiding of theory, qualitative research strategies, and sociopolitical consciousness for interacting with and gathering knowledge from young Mexicanas" (p. 643). She draws from CRT, Chicana feminisms, and the scholarship of women of Color in her use of *trenzas y mestizaje* as "a technique for advancing cross-disciplinary study, as well as reforming disciplinary canons, one that scholars can look to for illuminating cultural knowledge, its meanings, images, and practices" (p. 646). Her thinking is inspired by culture, religion, multiplicity (identities, realities, experiences, histories, and values), and their insectionality in the lives of Chicanas/Latinas. Delgado Bernal (2001) also reveals her application of a *mestiza* consciousness:

> [It] allowed me to better understand the lives of the students I interviewed and to organize and analyze my data in ways that are uncommon in the field of education . . . to include how a student balances, negotiates, and draws from her bilingualism, biculturalism, commitment to communities, and spiritualities in relationship to her education. (p. 627)

Her analysis of individual and focus-group interviews resulted in a counternarrative that recasted deficit language and images with declarations of the positive and empowering nature of bicultural and bilingualism. It also called for border crossing, where "borderlands refers to the geographical, emotional, and/or psychological space occupied by mestizas, and it serves as a metaphor for the condition of living, between spaces, cultures, and languages" (p. 632). Critical feminisms offer original and authentic lenses, detailing lives in which language and literacy are essential.

CRITICAL PEDAGOGY

When critical theorizing is practiced in the field of education as an approach to teaching, it is called critical pedagogy. Critical pedagogy, like other critical notions, has evolved over time and defies a single starting point or definition. Freire declares that teaching is a political act, one that should represent and respect multiple readings/writings of the world. He believed that teachers should envisage their role as educators and agents of social change and transformation by adopting and adapting a humanizing pedagogy that enhances an evolving critical consciousness:

> The method is, in fact, the external form of consciousness manifest in acts, which takes on the fundamental property of consciousness—its intentionality. The essence of consciousness is being with the world, and this behavior is permanent and unavoidable. Accordingly, consciousness is in essence a "way towards" something apart from itself, outside itself, which surrounds it and which it apprehends by means of its ideational capacity. Consciousness is thus defined by definition as a method, in the most general sense of the word. (Freire, 1993, p. 51)

To support intellectual development, Freire suggested that people should be taught how to help themselves or educate themselves about their reality. Although Freire and his supporters argue that there is no "method," Lyra's (1996) text, *As Quarenta horas de Angicos: Una Experiência Pioneira de Educacão,* describes a process. Lyra argues that the roles of dialogue and of establishing a relationship of mutual respect and exchange among teachers and students are key to Friere's pedagogy.

Shor (1980, 1987) has applied Freire's principles in his research, which ranges from critical literacy theory, to CWS, to postcolonialism, to the intersection of race and gender issues with social class. Shor's (1999) thinking is best captured in his response to the question: "What is critical literacy?":

> We are what we say and do. The way we speak and are spoken to help shape us into the people we become. . . . [T]hough language is fateful in teaching us what kind of people to become and what kind of society to make, discourse is not destiny. . . . This is where critical literacy begins, for questioning power relations, discourses, and identities in a world not yet finished, just, or humane. (p. 1)

Macedo, a frequent coauthor with Freire (1987, 2002), voices concern over the way that many U.S. teachers have attempted to use Freireian theory and pedagogy, constituting what he labels as the "methodology fetish." Macedo encourages U.S. educators to adopt an anti-method stance that "forces us to view dialogue as a form of social praxis so that the sharing of experiences is informed by reflection and political action" (p. 8).

Other scholars and educators, including Michael Apple, Stanley Arnowitz, Michelle Fine, Antonio Darder, Henry Giroux, bell hooks, Hilary Janks, Joe Kincheloe, Michele Knobel, Colin Lankshear, Alan Luke, Carmen Luke, Peter McLaren, Shirley Sternberg, and Lois Weis, among others, endorse critical pedagogy. Giroux (1999), for example, suggests that critical pedagogy seeks to

1. Create new forms of knowledge through its emphasis on breaking down disciplines and creating interdisciplinary knowledge.
2. Raise questions about the relationships between the margins and centers of power in schools and is concerned about how to provide a way of reading history as part of a larger project of reclaiming power and identity, particularly as these are shaped around the categories of race, gender, class, and ethnicity.
3. Reject the distinction between high and popular culture so as to make curriculum knowledge responsive to the everyday knowledge that constitutes peoples' lived histories differently.
4. Illuminate the primacy of the ethical in defining the language that teachers and others use to produce particular cultural practices. (np)

Additionally, McLaren (2004) writes that critical pedagogy supports Marxism, is nonviolent, and supports social democracy. He believes that critical pedagogy also "advocates a multiracial and anti-imperialist social movement dedicated to opposing racism, capitalism (both in private property and state property forms), sexism, heterosexism, hierarchies based on social class, as well as other forms of oppression" (McLaren, 2004, np). Kincheloe (2004) maintains that critical pedagogy is grounded on a social and educational vision of justice and equality, constructed on the belief that education is inherently political, and dedicated to the alleviation of human suffering.

Critical Language and Literacy Pedagogy

Freire maintained that it is important to understand "the oppressed's reality, as reflected in the various forms of cultural production—language, art, music—[which] leads to a better comprehension of the cultural expression through which people articulate their rebelliousness against the dominant" (P. Freire & Macedo, 1987, p. 137). He understood the tremendous role of critical consciousness in helping to shape language: "Language is also culture. Language is the mediating force of knowledge; but it is also knowledge itself" (P. Freire & Macedo, 1987, p. 53). He also recognized and supported the legitimacy and use of the languages of oppressed groups, often referred to as "bastardizations" of official or standard languages. Further, he believed that reading and writing are continuous processes where consciously reading and writing the world supports the transformation of the processes themselves and the world they are describing. He writes, "this dynamic movement is central to the literacy process" (Freire, 1987, p. 35).

Hall (1980) also recognizes that there are many ways to read the word and the world. Language is just one way—albeit a very important way—to communicate meaning. For example, when a message is being communicated to a listener/reader, that message must be coded/encoded/decoded in concert with the sender's understanding of the perceptions and expectations of the receiver. Hall identifies three distinctive readings/decodings of text: (1) dominant (hegemonic) reading, where the reader accepts the dominant or preferred meaning; (2) negotiated reading, where the reader partially accepts the dominant or preferred meaning; and (3) oppositional (counter-hegemonic) reading, where the reader rejects the dominant or preferred meaning and creates a new meaning that reflects the cultural and contextual systems of knowing that inform his/her life.

Hall also recognizes that what is understood, or perceived as naturalistic discourse, is not all natural: "it would be more appropriate to define the typical discourse . . . not as naturalistic, but as *naturalized*: not grounded in nature but producing nature as a sort of guarantee of its truth" (Hall, 1980, p. 75, italics in original). He does not claim, however, that all interpretations are valid, because meaning cannot be simply "private" and "individual" (p. 135). Further, he reasons, "an essential, true, original meaning is an illusion. No such previously natural moment of true meaning, untouched by codes of social relations of production and reading exists" (Hall, 1984, p. 2). Hall cautions that "meaning is a social production, a practice. The world has to be *made to mean*. Language and symbolization is the means by which meaning is produced" (Hall, 1982, p. 67, italics in original). If we accept that language is multi-referential and that relations and contexts influence language and literacy development, then cognitive-only or cognitive-primary explanations of literacy are inadequate. Also, Berhoff (1987) writes, "language is the means to a critical consciousness, which, in turn, is the means of conceiving of change and making choices to bring about further transformations" (p. xv). Language is a powerful tool in justifying and sustaining oppression.

Littlejohn and Hicks (2006) characterize language as part of larger structures of control. We agree, and submit that domains of power help control acceptance and the valuing of official or sanctioned languages over others. McCarty et al. (2005) point out that recognition of the many languages that make up the world often occludes or tends to "sanitize the underlying processes of cultural, economic, social, and political displacement that lead to language loss—what some scholars have labeled *linguistic genocide* or *linguicide*" (p. 2, italics in original). They acknowledge that, too often, the ideological basis of education—from preparation to curriculum to instruction to evaluation—uses the ideas and the language of the colonizer to sustain domination.

Extending Critical Pedagogy

Critical pedagogy, though mindful, sensitive, and respectful of the needs of all groups, has been extended and refined by scholars of Color and feminists. An explanation and application of CRT to education can be found in Tate's (1997) comprehensive review. Researchers have adopted CRT to more adequately address the historical and present-day contexts of race, racism, and oppression. Solórzano, Ceja, and Yosso (2000), for example, stress that CRT in education "simultaneously attempts to foreground race and racism in the research as well as challenge the traditional paradigms, methods, texts, and separate discourse on race, gender, and class by showing how these social constructs intersect to impact on communities of Color" (p. 63). Ladson-Billings and Donner (2005) promote CRT as a theoretical position that offers a "new analytic rubric for considering difference and inequality [and] . . . creating and passionately engaging in new visions of scholarship to do the work that ultimately will serve people and lead to human liberation" (p. 291). CRT deconstructs education's discourse, where color imagery, code words, and euphemisms point to unstated presumptions, myths, and stock stories about people of Color (Delgado & Stefancic, 2001).

Grande (2000a) also addresses pedagogical concerns within "the development of a new Red Pedagogy, or one that is historically grounded in American Indian intellectualism, politically centered in issues of sovereignty and tribal self-determination, and inspired by the religious and spiritual traditions of American Indian peoples" (p. 468). Her approach includes:

> 1) the quest for sovereignty and the dismantling of global capitalism as its political focus; (2) Indigenous knowledge as its epistemological foundation; (3) the Earth as its spiritual center; and (4) tribal and traditional ways of life as its sociocultural frame of reference. (Grande, 2000b, p. 355)

Deloria (1970, 1983, 1994) and other scholars who have sought to revolutionize Indigenous education inform Grande's position.

Romeo (2002) posits that Indigenous scholars worldwide seek self-determination, "reclaiming and revaluing of Indigenous languages, cultures, and 'consciousness' as a means of empowering and improving the educational success of Native students" (p. 250). Using narratives, she describes the educational events in the lives of young Native scholars who experience cultural dissonance within higher education. Smith (2005) voices similar sentiments as she identifies the central educational issues of the Indigenous community: "epistemic self-determination that includes language and culture and the challenges of generating schooling approaches from a different epistemological basis" (p. 94).

There are risks to adopting a curriculum from non-Western epistemological and cultural basis, according to Indigenous scholar Kaomea, a native Hawaiian. Indigenous scholars take offense with how non-Indigenous folk attempt to represent the history and culture of Indigenous people. Kaomea (2005) presents a case study of the use of an Indigenous studies curriculum by non-Indigenous educators in response to Hawai'i's passage of a 1978 constitutional amendment, which mandated that Native Hawaiian studies be taught, but left instruction to the classroom teacher. Most classroom teachers have not studied Hawaiian culture, language, and religions, and thus, they have brought limited knowledge to their classrooms. Kaomea argues that a curriculum "without accompanying structural changes in school personnel and community power relations" will not dismantle colonial discourses (p. 24). She argues that the responsibility to make changes should begin with the Indigenous people, who, working with allies, can restructure and revolutionize the educational systems in which their children are taught.

Likewise, Hermes (2005) comments that culture cannot be "institutionalized," but must be addressed along with a revolutionizing of the structure and content in the current educational system. Barnhardt and Kawagley (2005) propose a collaboration between Indigenous epistemological, cultural, and linguistic efforts and Western thinking. Ismail and Cazden (2005) seek a common ground for Indigenous scholars and educators and their non-Indigenous allies to address the needs in Indigenous education.

There has been an important shift and critique of Whiteness in critical pedagogy (Cowlishaw & Frankenberg, 1999; Frankenberg & Mani, 1993; Gallagher, 1995; McIntyre, 1997; Rodriguez, 2000; Trainor, 2005). McIntyre's (1997) study of how White teachers understand race articulates a particular way of talking about race, which she labels "White talk." She describes it as "talking uncritically with/ to other Whites, all the while resisting critique and massaging each other's racist attitudes, beliefs, and actions" (pp. 145–146). Her research suggests that a greater acknowledgment of White consciousness and the power and privilege of Whiteness is needed. Feagin and van Ausdale (2001) support McIntyre's observation, writing, "Today, the majority of White Americans seem to be in denial about the seriousness of racial prejudices, emotions, and discrimination in their own lives, the lives of their friends and relatives, and the larger society" (p. 29). Acknowledgment of Whiteness and its inherent power and privileges is an important step toward equity, social justice, and democracy in language and literacy research. Ferber (2007) also calls for the inclusion of discussions on privilege to balance the focus on oppression, noting "oppression and privilege operate hand in hand . . . one cannot exist without the other. Privilege operates on the basis of a variety of social locations, including race, ethnicity, gender, and sexual orientation" (p. 266).

Yosso (2005a) takes a different path to champion, validate, and defend the importance of cultural knowledge as part of critical pedagogy. She opposes the way in which scholars have used Bourdieu's notion of cultural capital in a deficit manner in their descriptions of the lack of cultural capital of non-Whites. She challenges this idea by adapting Oliver and Shapiro's (1995) idea of community cultural wealth and describes six forms of wealth that support the knowledge that students of Color bring to schools: aspirational, familial, linguistic, navigational, resistance, and social capital. Yosso argues that these forms of capital should be used for academic success.

Critical Feminist Pedagogies

Feminist pedagogy is not singular, but instead represents multiple feminist pedagogies that share some commonalities with critical pedagogy, including an emphasis on action, dialogue, participation, reflection, and voice as part of learning, especially among marginalized groups. Critical feminist pedagogies have evolved from being centered on the ideas and stances of White women (Coffey & Delamont, 2000; Gonick, 2003; Luke & Gore, 1992; Walkerdine, 1990) to include the lives, experiences, and concerns of women of Color from the periphery: Black feminists (Collins, 1990, 1998, 2000; Dillard, 2000; hooks, 1994; Omolade, 1993), Chicanas (Delgado Bernal, 1998, 2001; Sandoval, 1998), Chicanas/Mexicanas (Elenes, Gonzalez, Delgado Bernal, & Villenas, 2001), Latinas (Medina, 2004), and Indigenous women (Emberley, 1996; González, 2001; Hernández-Avila, 1997). Davis, a student of Marcuse, recognized that critical theories can incorporate race, gender, and class consciousness, and that "the most effective versions of feminism acknowledge the various ways gender, class, race, and sexual orientation inform each other" (Davis & James, 1998, p. 304).

Collins's (1990, 2000) description of Black Feminist Theory suggests that there are important points of difference among feminisms. She observes that Black women have shared their knowledge and evolving critical consciousness in what she identifies as "safe spaces" (p. 100), where subjugated and oppositional knowledges are welcomed and affirmed in song, fiction, and poetry. Similarly, Delgado Bernal (2001) draws on the growing body of Chicana/Mexicana/Latina scholarship to help frame her understandings of Chicana feminisms and *mestiza* consciousness. She writes, "Chicana feminist pedagogies refers to culturally specific ways of organizing teaching and learning in informal sites such as the homeways that embrace Chicana and *Mexicana* ways of knowing and extend beyond formal schooling" (p. 624). She notes that *mestiza* literally means "a woman of mixed ancestry, especially of Native American, European, and African backgrounds . . . [and] has come to mean a new Chicana consciousness that straddles cultures, races, languages, nations, sexualities, and spiritualities" (p. 626). In response to critical pedagogies, she suggests, "The pedagogies of the home extend the existing discourse on critical pedagogies by putting cultural knowledge and language at the forefront to better understand lessons from the home space and local communities" (p. 624). She envisages a time when racial/ethnic epistemologies and critical consciousness will be used to improve instruction and academic performance.

Grande (2000a) offers a historical and etymological discussion of the term *mestizaje* and supports Anzaldua's (1987) promotion of *mestiza* consciousness, Delgado Bernal's (1998) feminist Chicana consciousness, and the idea of *mestizaje* espoused by Darder, Torres, and Gutierrez (1997) and Valle and Torres (1995). Gonzáles (2001) sees *mestizaje* as "a consciousness of an ethical commitment to egalitarian social relations in the everday political sphere of culture" (p. 646). Grande prefers to portray *mestizaje* as a separate tradition, not to be co-opted by critical theorists who wish to address the socially constructed notion of multisubjectivity.

Summary

As the bedrock of critical theorizing, critical consciousness points to the importance of acknowledging all forms of injustice. Historically, dominant groups have tried to persuade other groups that the dominant group is the superior group by exploiting their racial/ethnic, gender, and class differences. Contemporary evolutions of criticality include racial and feminist theories that acknowledge intersecting oppression. Critical race-conscious theorists address race as a social construct and understand it as a lived reality that is sustained by power elites. Likewise, critical feminisms deconstruct the ways in which languages and literacies are used by power elites to control images of gender, values, and beliefs.

Critical pedagogy has sought to translate critical theorizing into educational praxis. It seeks to honor and respect humankind and the multiple cultures, knowledges, languages, and literacies of learners. It encourages educators to acknowledge the hegemonic forces that seek to control individuals and groups through research, standardization, and testing. In contrast, critically conscious language and literacy research aims to examine and critique dominant ideologies, policies, and practices that are unjust, as well as the mischaracterization of cultures, knowledges, languages, and literacies. We suggest that critical language and literacy scholars should draw from multiple sources of critical theorizing.

CHAPTER 4

Critical Methodologies and Methods

Theory, then, is a set of knowledges. . . . [I]t is vital that we occupy theorizing space. . . . By bringing our own approaches and methodologies, we transform that theorizing space.
—Gloria E. Anzaldúa, 1990, p. xxv

Our view of critical methodology (the philosophies that underlie research) and methods (the processes and techniques of research) recognizes that inquiry begins with the critical consciousness of the researcher. Critical consciousness underpins research methods; informs questions; guides data collection; and is applied in analysis, interpretation, and recommendations. We began this book by examining some of the epistemological roots and routes of critical theorizing and its current manifestations. Now we turn to the ways in which critical consciousness informs methodology. As Marcuse (1973) noted: "the real field of knowledge is not the given facts about things as they are, but the critical evaluation of them as a prelude to passing beyond their given form" (p. 145). The methodology used in criticality has global roots and routes that are seldom recognized in the West. As our history of ideas illustrates, no group of philosophers, theorists, or scientists has established a methodology or set of methods to discover truth.

It is believed that the dialectical method began in Asia with I Ching's notion of yin and yang, followed by the thinking of Lao Tzu. Although most often traced to the Greeks (Aristotle, Heraclitus, Socrates), Western ideas of dialectics as a way of seeking truth also can be found in the thinking of the Aztec and Lakota nations. If you'll recall the central Western figures of CT, Kant (1784) believed that critique should challenge concepts, questions, and underlying assumptions, as well as political or social interests. His essays were conduits through which he expressed his thinking, as did his successors. Hegel also used the dialectical method, which he borrowed from Fichte, to explain his understanding of truth. He was followed by Marx and Engels, who developed their theory of dialectical materialism. *Dialectics* is a critical examination of an argument, opinion, or statement that uses logic to resolve a conflict between two contradictory or interacting ideas. The process involves presenting the "truths" on both sides while disproving one in favor of another; it is typically represented as thesis–antithesis–synthesis. Sherman (1976) lists several rules of the dialectical method: interconnections, change, unity, quantity and quality, and negation of the negation. Fairclough (1999) suggests that the process consists of four distinct stages:

> identification of a problem, identification of what it is in the network of social practices that gives rise to the problem, consideration of whether and how the problem is functional in sustaining the system (e.g., whether it works ideologically), and identification of real possibilities within the domain of social life in question for overcoming the problem. (p. 7)

Critically conscious research represents multiple, intersecting, and interdisciplinary principles and processes. There is no singular history, theory, or methodology that is common to all criticality, nor are methods reducible to a single set of steps, guidelines, and criteria (Bronner, 2002; Quantz, 1992). Critical methods, however, do address and challenge "taken-for-granted assumptions about objectivity, validity, reliability, and who should be involved in the research process" (Gitlin & Russell, 1994, p. 181). Some language and literacy researchers/scholars openly reveal that their work adopts a critical stance; others prefer to have their texts unveil their position; and still others frame their research to discuss issues that are germane to critical theory/ies.

Kincheloe and McLaren (2005) observe, "Inquiry that aspires to the name *critical* must be connected to an attempt to confront the injustice of a particular society or public sphere within the society" (p. 291, italics in the original). Kincheloe (1998) offers a general description of the "essence" of critical research:

> the "critical" aspect of critical research assumes that the inequalities of contemporary society need to be addressed and that the world would be a better place if such unjust realities could be changed. . . . [W]e explore the world . . . for the purpose of exposing this injustice,

developing practical ways to change it, and identifying sites and strategies by which transformation can be accomplished. (p. 1191)

Critically conscious language and literacy researchers aim to deconstruct, demystify, and articulate the relationship among disparate beliefs, thoughts, and actions, as well as to illustrate how these ideas influence equity and social justice.

CRITICAL QUALITATIVE METHODS

Critical consciousness punctuates the methodology and methods that we present with examples from critical language and literacy research. Carspecken and Apple (1992) discuss the differences between critical qualitative research and other forms of field-based inquiry. They acknowledge that critical researchers have political intentions to transform social inequalities: "the critical approach . . . is distinguished first of all in terms of the motivation of the researcher and the questions that are posed" (p. 512). The question(s) guides: observations, data collection, development of categories, coding of units, links between categories, selecting compelling examples, framework for analysis and interpretation, and presentation of data. In what follows, we discuss critical qualitative methods, critical discourse analysis, and critical ethnography. We also briefly examine and critique critical policy analysis and CRT methods.

Critical Discourse Analysis

Critical discourse analysis (CDA) is a form of discourse analysis that is inspired by the thinking of Derrida, Habermas, Gramsci, and Marx, among others. Bloome and Carter (2005) submit that, historically, the term *discourse* was used as a verb. However, more recently, the term is used as a noun and a modifier. They offer the following brief definition of *critical discourse analysis:* "a set of approaches to discourse analysis focusing on power relations. The models of power, understandings of language, culture, and social processes, and foci of analysis, varies across approaches" (Bloome & Carter, 2005, p. 1). Matthews (2005) also suggests that CDA is applied to a diverse set of practices, including "speech act theory and pragmatics, conversation analysis, discursive psychology, the ethnography of communication, interactional sociolinguistics, narrative analysis, and critical discourse analysis" (p. 207). Fairclough and Wodak (1997) identified several theoretical approaches to CDA: French discourse analysis, critical linguistics, social semiotics, sociocultural change and change in discourse, sociocognitive studies, discourse-historical method, reading analysis, and the Dusiburg School. He also suggested that CDA consists of three dimensions simultaneously: language text (spoken or written, or visual messages), discourse practices, and sociocultural practices.

Fairclough and Wodak's (1997) research has dominated the field. They describe the distinction between discourse analysis and CDA as:

> Critical discourse analysis sees discourse—language use in speech and writing—as a form of "social practice." Describing discourse as social practice implies a dialectical relationship between a particular discursive event and the situation(s), institution(s), and social structure(s) which frame it. A dialectical relationship is a two-way relationship: the discursive event is shaped by situations, institutions and social structures, but it also shapes them. (p. 55)

Further, they write, "any part of any language text, spoken or written, is simultaneously constituting representations, relations, and identities" (p. 275). CDA studies may be applied to government documents, media, textbooks, and electronic databases.

As one of its main goals, CDA "takes the part of the underprivileged and tries to show up the linguistic means used by the privileged to stabilize or even to intensify inequities in society" (Meyer, 2000, p. 30). It emphasizes anti-racism and anti-bias in research, albeit not from a critical race perspective (van Dijk, 1991, 1993; Wodak, 1996). Van Dijk (1991) examines how discourse is used in the media to sustain racial stereotypes, not unlike the early work in CCCS. Wallace (1999) suggests that CDA limits critique, as does Janks (2005), whose work extends notions of critique to praxis. Matthews (2005) melds discourse analysis with critical pedagogy and "explores how dominant discourses work through multiple texts to show how identities are established and how knowledges and understandings are taken up as history, politics, justice, and 'truth'" (p. 206). We share examples of CDA in critical language and literacy studies below.

CDA in Language and Literacy Research

Rogers (2002a, 2002b, 2004) offers a rare glimpse into the evolution of a critically conscious researcher as she applies CDA in her research. Her early studies (2002a, 2002b) draw on her dissertation research and detail her work with one African American family, including its extended family members. A later study (Rogers, 2004) is based on a series of interviews that she conducted among African American adult literacy learners in which she attempted to test theories from her earlier studies. Collectively, these studies reveal shifts in Rogers's definition and description of critical literacy; use, understanding, and ownership of CDA; and use, understanding, and knowledge of the scholarship of African Americans.

Trainor (2005) examines White identity and racism among English majors using CDA. Her work is inspired by Morrison's (1992) notion of race as metaphorical. She applies CDA as a framework for analysis of how White students talk about race in courses that focus on multicultural literature and understanding. Trainor's analysis of "White talk" highlights a way of reading the word and the world that is found in classroom discourses about race. She acknowledges that she is an insider, which gives her access to "White talk," because she, like her particpants, is White, middle-class, female, from the Midwest, and raised in a racially homogeneous community. She envisages herself as an outsider in her teacher education classes, given her "commitment to anti-racist pedagogy" (Trainor, 2005, p. 149). She shows that the students' claims of "just being White" are problematic by looking closely at how their "characterizations stem from our equating White discourse with White identity and privilege, an equation that ultimately creates for students a coherent identity position that elides important questions about how identities actually work" (Trainor, 2005, p. 145). She writes that not all White people use this type of talk, or talk this way about race. Her findings evince an attempt by White students to embrace notions of White innocence and White victimization, which they express through feelings of discomfort and a lack of experience in a multiracial and multicultural world.

Burns and Morrell (2005) also explain and offer ideas for the use of CDA in literacy research. They argue that literacy researchers must do more than "understand the role of discourse in social reproduction. Literacy researchers are also called to intervene in, challenge, and deconstruct oppressive discursive structures to facilitate more empowering engagements with institutionalized discourses or the creation of alternative ones" (p. 132). They describe the application of CDA as a methodological, analytical, pedagogical, and policy tool in literacy research.

Critical Ethnography

Our stance on critical consciousness as part of a global history of ideas acknowledges Trueba's (1999) suggestion that it is possible to trace critical ethnography to Francisco Tenamazile and his 1542 defense of "the rights of all Indians" (p. 591). Trueba argues that

> critical ethnography must advocate for the oppressed by (1) document-ing the nature of oppression, (2) documenting the process of empower-ment . . . , (3) accelerating the conscientization of the oppressed and the oppressors . . . , (4) sensitizing the research community to the implica-tions of research for the quality of life . . . , and (5) reaching a higher level of understanding of the historical, political, sociological and eco-nomic factors supporting the abuse of power and oppression. (p. 128)

He believes that critical ethnography should be conducted with an understanding of how hegemonic forces have shaped history, with a commitment to praxis and emancipatory action.

Quantz (1992) presents a brief and more recent chronology of critical ethnography. He identifies five recurring themes in critical eth-nographic projects: knowledge, values, society, culture, and history. He places critical ethnography within the broader notion of a critical dis-course that attempts to re-present the "'culture,' the 'consciousness,' or the 'lived experiences' of people living in asymmetrical power rela-tions" (p. 448). He also stresses that critical ethnography seeks eman-cipation and democracy, and he points to the importance of retaining the synergism between theory and method in critical ethnography: "[M]ethod is fully embedded in theory and theory is expressed in method. . . . [M]ethod must never be reduced to technique" (p. 449).

Carspecken (1996) presents a helpful theoretical background for novices in the field and resists the temptation to offer a compre-hensive chronology or exhaustive review of philosophical theories that underpin critical ethnography. He incorporates the thinking of key figures of CT, although he does not cite the contributions of any women or people of Color. He posits:

> We are all concerned about social inequalities, and we direct our work toward positive social change. We also share a concern with social theory and some of the basic issues it has struggled with since the nineteenth century . . . the nature of social structure, power, culture, and human agency. We use our research, in fact, to refine social theory rather than merely to describe social life. (p. 3)

A central part of his thinking involves addressing the issues of power, language, and truth. Carspecken differentiates between a critical value orientation and a critical epistemology, noting that the former includes values that define critical orientations, whereas the latter is holistic and seeks to understand human experiences that are grounded in an effort to communicate. He also calls for interrogating communication, intersubjectivity, and the entirety of human experiences.

Carspecken outlines a useful set of guidelines for conducting critical ethnography. A preliminary step includes creating a list of research questions and a list of specific items for study, and then examining the researcher's value orientations. Next, he suggests a five-stage approach to research: (1) compiling the primary record through the collection of monological data, (2) preliminary reconstructive analysis, (3) dialogical data generation, (4) discovering systems relations, and (5) using system relations to explain findings. He suggests that the preliminary and subsequent stages be followed in order. His work raises two concerns: First, his discussion dismisses much of what is at the heart of critical theorizing—including a clear commitment to addressing the needs of the oppressed, to social justice, and to educational equity. Second, his procedural steps appear too lock-step and are too focused on "getting the method right," as opposed to emphasizing democracy, liberation, or social justice.

Retrospectively, Foley (2001) offers a discussion of his own evolution as a critical ethnographer by reviewing the history of critical theorizing, acknowledging changes in its application by various subgroups of criticalists and identifying central components of application. He believes that "at least a year of fieldwork using the conventional ethnographic methods of participant observer, key informants, and interviewing" is fundamental to all critical ethnographic research (p. 472). Foley believes that reflexive investigators possess certain key assumptions, including an understanding that cultural reality is group- and context-specific, an acknowledgment that historical and social realities are partial, and an awareness of personal responsibility to portray other cultures, peoples, and realities accurately. In an autoethnographic sense, he discusses four specific types of ethnographic reflexivity that are used in ethnographic writing: confessional, theoretical, textual, and deconstructive.

Madison's (2005) scholarship, which is informed by philosophers and scholars from Socrates to Carspecken, adds her perspective and life experiences as a woman of Color living under oppression in the United States and traveling abroad as a U.S. citizen. She characterizes critical ethnography as "critical theory in action. Theory, when used as mode of interpretation, is a method, yet can be distinguished from method . . . when a set of concrete actions grounded by a specific scene is required to complete a task" (p. 15). She believes that critical ethnographers are morally and ethically bound to uphold the dignity of the process and the participants. Madison passionately argues that it is the moral and ethical responsibility of critical ethnographers "to address processes of unfairness or injustice within a particular lived domain" (p. 5). Likewise, Duncan (2005) believes that critical race ethnography offers "to take up the words of people of colour seriously . . . to allow these voices to inform how we approach our examination of the material conditions that are basic to and inextricably a part of lived experience" (p. 106). As with other forms of ethnography, critical race ethnography uses multiple techniques and data sources for analysis.

CRT Methodology and Methods

CRT scholars draw from multiple racial/ethnic epistemologies to situate their work and ask questions that challenge preconceived notions about the beliefs, values, knowledge, and ways of making meaning held by people of Color. Building upon the beliefs and traditions expressed by African American scholars and social activists, which are mentioned above, they seek to dismantle the discourse that surrounds race/ethnicity. They view discourse as a vehicle that is often used to disguise racial/ethnic bias through descriptions and assumptions about people of Color. Solórzano and Yosso (2002) argue that CRT methodology is theoretically grounded research that

1. foregrounds race and racism in all aspects of the research process;
2. challenges the traditional research paradigm, texts, and theories used to explain the experiences of people of Color;
3. offers a liberatory or transformative solution to racial, gender, and class subordination;
4. focuses on the racialized, gendered, and classed experiences of students of Color;
5. uses the interdisciplinary knowledge base of ethnic studies, women's studies, sociology, history, humanities, and the law to better understand the experiences of students of Color. (p. 24)

CRT accepts that experience and reflection upon experience are essential to understanding the effects of racial inequality (Pizarro, 1998). CRT's emancipatory and transformative stance emphasizes cultural and experiential knowledge through narratives and voice to examine race, racism, and power in society.

Scholars produce their own narratives as counterstories to the way in which cultures, lives, and the experiences of people of Color are depicted in mainstream and academic traditions. They use autobiography, biography, parables, stories, *testimonio*, and voice, infusing humor and allegory to expose hidden truths and to explicate and situate race, racism, and power within the experiences of people of Color without the need for interlopers, interlocutors, or interpreters of the "Other." They produce stories told from the position of people of Color living under racial oppression that contradict or oppose the assumptions and beliefs held by many Whites. Inherent in the narrative forms is voice, that is, the ability of a group to articulate its experience in ways that are unique to its members (Delgado & Stefancic, 2001). Their narratives are exceptionally detailed to help capture the richness of contexts and to include revisionist historical information, experiences, and explanations. Scholars also use storytelling to analyze and dispel myths, assumptions, and unfounded beliefs about people of Color (Delgado & Stefancic, 2000, p. xvii). The stories not only illustrate but also help contextualize experiences of oppression by asking deep and searching questions of the oppressor and the oppressed that cannot be solved by Western-Eurocentric theorizing.

Solórzano and Yosso (2001), for instance, use storytelling to "challenge the perceived wisdom at society's center by providing a context [for] understand[ing] and transform[ing] established belief systems" (p. 475). They explain that storytelling is a tool to "teach others that by combining elements from both the story and the current reality, one can construct another world that is richer than either the story or the reality alone" (p. 475). They begin by collecting, examining, and analyzing a host of concepts, ideas, and experiences, while using both theoretical sensitivity and cultural intuition. Next, they construct counternarratives following four steps that include (1) gathering data, (2) reviewing extant literature, (3) drawing on their professional experiences, and (4) reflecting on their personal experiences (p. 476). The idea of voice carries with it the notion that the groups' voices are especially qualified to tell their own stories, without essentializing their experiences to all group members. By way of contrast, many White language and literacy researchers self-identify by race, gender, or class, yet seldom do they deconstruct what these markers mean to them and how these identities shape their research, findings, and recommendations. Many also position themselves and their roles as transparent—"the ability of whiteness to disguise itself and become invisible" (Delgado & Stefancic, 2001, p. 156), whereas CRT scholars believe that in the United States, race is visible, tangible, and omnipresent, although racism can be overt, dysconscious, or unconscious.

CRT methodology also reveals the importance of language, literacy, and culture in the lives of people of Color and demonstrates the interwoven nature of language and literacy use as multidimensional, multicontextual, and multifaceted. This body of research explicates and validates the multiple consciousnesses and literacies that people of Color use in their lives. Equally important is acknowledging intersectionality in the lives of people of Color, which helps clarify how multidimensional identities are formed and how they are necessary for survival within and outside of our communities.

Critical Policy Analysis

Shaw (2004) explains that policy analysis consists of the following assumptions: single truth theory, researcher objectivity, and homogenization of participant experiences. She writes, "traditional policy analysis willfully ignores the inherently political nature of all research, and policy research in particular" (p. 58). Edmonson (2002) argues, "rather than focusing solely on the question of *what is*, the critical policy analyst asks, among others, *what has been*, *why*, and *what might be*" (p. 114, italics in the original). She examines policies related to reading research in the late 1990s, especially those related to the defunct America Reads program and the Reading Excellence Act, claiming that "educational policy and educational practices are never objective, technical matters. Instead they are always evaluative and political" (p. 118). Duncan (2005) supports the use of CRT as a lens for policy analysis in situations where literacy is understood as the property of Whites. He articulates that in the United States, there are long-standing and unresolved anxieties over Blackness and Whiteness and "between *property* rights and *human* rights . . . to maintain an unequal distribution of economic, social, and political resources that privileges white people over people of colour" (p. 95). In short, there is a long and troubling relationship between federal policies and literacy, underscored by social unrest and oppression based on race/ethnicity and social class.

CRITIQUES OF CRITICAL RESEARCH

Beyond the oft-mentioned idea of quantifying education, criticality is viewed as philosophical, interpretative, or rhetorical. As we have noted, the push for change in criticality has come from those who have lived under oppression, specifically people of Color and women. Their scholarship encourages researchers to adopt, recognize, respect, and value the critical consciousness of women and people of Color, which can expand opportunities for language and literacy researchers to engage in more explicit, accurate, and authentic understandings of racial/ethnic epistemologies, intersectionalities of difference, and domains of power in the lives of oppressed participants.

Grande (2000b), for example, argues that critical theorizing should be disentangled from narrowly defined Marxist perspectives if it is to be useful in educational research. She examines the intersections of American Indian epistemology and intellectualism and critical theory, arguing that "critical theories are often indiscriminately employed to explain the sociopolitical conditions of all marginalized peoples" (p. 46). She envisions more distinctive understandings of the resistance to oppression and the struggle for social justice by American Indians. Grande explains that tensions emerge around notions of identity, between describing and centering race/ethnicity as one form of difference and more fluid, postmodern descriptions of hybridism. She demystifies the popular use of hybridism, arguing against "the intersections at the borderlands," where "hybridity and all subjects are constructed as inherently transgressive" (p. 47).

Smith (1999) also presents a guide for thinking about and pursuing research among Indigenous peoples. However, as she notes, the word *research* is "one of the dirtiest words in the Indigenous world's vocabulary," in part because their lifeways have been misunderstood and misinterpreted by outsiders (p. 1). She argues, "Research is one of the ways in which the underlying code of imperialism and colonialism is both regulated and realized. It is regulated through the formal rules of individual scholarly disciplines and scientific paradigms, and the institutions that support them" (p. 8). Further, she articulates that from an Indigenous perspective, the research protocols of the West require "a cultural orientation, a set of values, a different conceptualization of such things as time, space and subjectivity, different and competing theories of knowledge, highly specialized forms of language, and structures of power" (p. 42). She declares that the very lives and ways of Indigenous people have been misappropriated within stories about researchers' journeys. Smith believes that it is important to understand, respect, and value Indigenous knowledge when conducting research and to recognize that Indigenous research methods may differ markedly from Western research methods, but are no less appropriate, important, or rigorous.

Smith (1999) challenges "insider" researchers to be aware that their individual experience/s cannot be essentialized as being reflective of an entire group's experience. She observes that Indigenous insiders face additional criteria among their own groups, especially from elders, that are beyond Western viewpoints. Smith poses important questions for researchers to consider when conducting research among Indigenous groups: "Whose research is it? Who owns it? Whose interests does it serve? Who will benefit from it? Who has designed its questions and framed its scope? Who will carry it out? Who will write it up? How will its results be disseminated?" (p. 10). Bishop (2005) articulates Maori people's concern about the researcher's position and suggests that researchers address issues of initiation, benefits, representation, legitimacy, and accountability (p. 112). Collectively, these criticisms foreground the importance of understanding criticality within this historical moment as the oppressed clarify epistemological principles and set forth guidelines for conducting research within racial/ethnic communities.

Insider/Outsider/Within

There are researchers who self-identify as both insiders and outsiders of the groups that participate in their research projects and who bring informed and respectful understandings of cultures, languages, and literacies to the project and process. As Ladson-Billings and Donner (2005) observe:

> the process of developing a worldview that differs from the dominant worldview requires active intellectual work on the part of the knower, because schools, society, and the structure and production of knowledge are designed to create individuals who internalize the dominant worldview and knowledge production and acquisition processes. (p. 258)

Duncan (2002a) and Tejeda (2004) conduct critical language and literacy research that uses an ethnic/racial "system of knowing" (Ladson-Billings, 2000, p. 257) that includes multiple perspectives.

Most White critical theorists dismissively describe themselves as White and as outsiders of the communities in which their research is conducted. On occasion some also describe themselves by gender, class, and language dominance. However, it is more common for White researchers to state that, because of their unique and unusually close relationships with and among their participants of Color, they possess an uncanny understanding of the lived experiences, culture, and language of their participants and concomitant empathy for the oppression and racism experienced by their participants; in other words, they describe themselves as "outsiders within." Collectively, generic descriptors have become the unacknowledged standpoints for analyses, interpretation, and discussions of students of Color and their literacy needs, without any interrogation of the Whiteness that underpins the theorizing and methods of the researchers. Brookfield (2003) draws on Marcuse's notion of repressive tolerance, arguing that Eurocentrism used in this way "masks its repression behind the facade of open even-handedness" while simultaneously positioning the views held by scholars of Color as alternative, if not exotic (p. 502).

Research that is so positioned does not address the historical, social, political, and linguistic contexts or domains of power in the lives of participants. Perhaps unwittingly, in an effort to demonstrate "fairness" and to support "identity" laced with critical pronouncements, the researcher's power to "name" marginalizes the participants' ethnic/racial and linguistic knowledges and re-centers Western-Eurocentric ways of knowing, gendered ideas, and linguistic dominance. Carol Lee (2003) suggests that it is imperative that we question "what it means to understand individuals within their participation in ethnic cultural practices as well as within the broader institutional social, economic, and political relationships that are part of a multiethnic democratic society" (p. 3). As noted, notions of hybridity and fluidity have replaced complex discussions of race, class, and gender; studies by some Whites tend to deny the importance of race by replacing race with identity. Given these shortcomings, many cultural outsiders often reveal a limited understanding of the very data they present, data that cultural insiders may read and interpret very differently.

As criticality continues to evolve, Collins (2000) suggests replacing traditional categories of analysis with categories that fully capture "human relationships that transcend the legitimate differences" (p. 333). She believes that in the academy, traditional categories of analysis need to be reconsidered by challenging the dichotomies of differences (Black/White, male/female, and so on) and replacing those categories with categories that capture "fully human relationships that transcend the legitimate differences" (p. 333). She suggests that we recognize traditional categories of analysis as part of a system of oppression and forego attempts to create a hierarchical ordering of suffering. We have adopted and adapted her ideas in the review and critique of critical language and literacy research that we present in the following chapters.

Summary

We have extended the idea of roots and routes to a review of how methodologies inform critical language and literacy research. Critical consciousness should exhibit an awareness of personal beliefs, values, and viewpoints in framing research; sociohistorical contexts that sustain oppression, especially oppression under which participants live and learn; dominant ideologies and policies that define the languages and literacies in the lives of participants; and ways in which recommendations for social justice can be positively implemented.

We believe that Collins's (1990, 2000) model offers an appreciatively important understanding of how domains of power sustain systems of oppression. Her model moves beyond the singular identity markers that are typically employed in the academy and interrogates the intersectionality of oppressions within domains of power (structural and disciplinary, hegemonic, and interpersonal). It is a more sophisticated and complex model that is well suited for representing multiple oppressions, intersecting realities, and domains of power.

CHAPTER 5

Critically Conscious Language and Literacy Research: Structural and Disciplinary Domains of Power

Theory is always a response to a particular context.
—Lawrence Grossberg, 1994, p. 5

We use Collins's (1990, 2000) model of analysis, which recognizes that multiple and intersecting forms of oppression are sustained by the matrix of domination (structural, disciplinary, hegemonic, and interpersonal). Critically conscious language and literacy scholars bring a sociohistoric perspective to their research. Leistyna, Woodrum, and Sherblom (1996) define a *sociohistorical lens* as working "from the assumption that we are never independent of the social and historical forces that surround us. . . . [W]e all inherit beliefs, values, and ideologies that need to be critically understood and transformed where necessary" (p. 343). In this chapter, we review and critique critical consciousness language and literacy research that tackles structural and disciplinary domains of power.

This body of research reflects multiple domains within politics and government agencies, religion, economics, and curricular materials in schools and communities. In addition, we recognize language as an identity marker because, in all countries, official languages have the privilege to retain, sustain, and maintain power, and to reproduce inequalities through language use. We also include immigrant status as an identity marker under which people experience oppression.

STRUCTURAL DOMAIN OF POWER

Collins (2000) characterizes the structural domain of power as "a constellation of organized practices in employment, government, education, law, business, and housing that work to maintain an unequal and unjust distribution of social resources" (p. 301). In each study, there are opportunities for researchers to address intersections of oppression sustained within multiple structural domains, albeit our focus is on educational systems and areas where structural domains of power obstruct or impede equity and social justice. Historically, alarms have sounded over language and literacy crises in public schools (Willis, 1997). The latest crisis emerged in part as a response to a series of reviews of extant literature that focused on beginning reading instruction and subsequent reviews of language use and instruction. In the current crisis, institutional structures and disciplinary practices sustain race/ethnic, class, gender, and linguistic oppression. Collins (2003) reminds us that "whether we benefit or not, we all live within institutions that reproduce race, class, and gender oppression" (p. 339). As language and literacy researchers and educators, we are all part of the process, and, potentially, the solution.

Politics and Government Agencies

Bacchi (2000) and Gale (2000) present overarching frameworks for understanding discourse in politics, using CDA and critical policy analysis to characterize and analyze the language use of officials and official documents, respectively. They note that policy-as-discourse examines language use to make and clarify meaning and to promote someone's purpose (political, legal, or social) for change. Gale (2000), for example, reviews the use of governmental power and discourse that supports specific agendas, tracing who discusses, who gets heard, who does not get heard, and under what circumstances. His study examines discourses surrounding a specific policy of Australian higher education between 1987 and 1996 and identifies six discourse strategies: "trading, bargaining, arguing, stalling, manoeuvring, and lobbying" (p. 60). He concludes that, although the results appear to be consensual, in reality, they represent a struggle for power among stakeholders.

N. Fernandez (2001) explicates changes in the discourse around issues of race in Cuba during the late 20th century. She observes that African slaves who were brought to work within the colonial system were oppressed, and their progeny continue to be oppressed and treated as inferior today. Fernandez reveals that a goal of the Cuban political restructuring of society in 1959 was the elimination of racial discrimination. Racism has not been prevented under socialism, or under what she refers to as "Cubanness," that is, Cuba's racial mixture (p. 129). Despite the government's official stance that there are no racial differences among citizens, Cuba has conceded that there is racial prejudice. Fernandez identifies the discourse used in popular media and academic circles as being more vocal about the existence of racism; a change from the past, when there was a "hegemonic silence" within Cuba about race (p. 120). She suggests that the shift has come about as the economy of Cuba has become more stable.

Shannon's (2000) analysis of the rhetoric of reading instruction also recasts changes in literacy as part of the outgrowth of broad political and societal shifts in the United States, or, as he puts it, "struggles for recognition" (p. 93). He identifies five points of view (conservative, neoconservative, neoliberal, liberal, and radical democratic) in response to literacy education. His summative comments encourage researchers to continue questioning and challenging shifts in the field, especially those that appear to be responses to one view over another.

Janks (2005) uses CDA to describe, deconstruct, and reconstruct advertisements from the United Nations High Commission for Refugees. She maintains that the advertisements are political, yet seek to neutralize refugee status within "discourses of assimilation and sameness" (p. 31). She uses Critical Language Awareness (CLA) to focus on the notion that "the relationship between language and power is a resource for thinking about the ways in which a text has been constructed, moment by moment, as the writer or speaker selects from a range of possible language, visual, and gestural options" (p. 34). Janks understands that the selection of discourse is purposeful and is supportive of a dominant ideology. She draws on Thompson's (1990) "five modes of operation of ideology: reification, legitimation, dissimulation, unification, and fragmentation" for her analysis of the advertisements (p. 37). She encourages teachers to help students deconstruct text to "understand how texts work to produce effects and how texts can be redesigned to produce different, more positive effects" (p. 33).

Case, Ndura, and Righettini (2005) show that the use of English as the official U.S. language and its primacy in schools is problematic. They posit that language and literacy instruction in the United States is under tremendous pressure to conform to an invisible standard where "white European American culture within U.S. schools is maintained through the selection of texts, the creation of public policy around programs, scripted reading programs, language planning policy, and high-stakes testing" (p. 375). Lomawaima and Mc-Carty (2002) express similar concerns, writing, "buried in the rhetoric of standards and accountability is the fact that the mandates to standardize testing are not accompanied by parallel mandates to standardize the economic and social investment in children subjected to the tests" (p. 298). Rumberger and Gándara (2004) also describe the achievement gap between English Language Learners (ELLs) and their English-speaking counterparts by exposing the consistent discourse, described as a "policy of inequality," in California's governmental stance toward ELLs' pursuit of education. They document legislation that requires students to pass the California High School Exit Exam (CHSEE), which is only available in English. This kind of inequity supports Freire's contention that "only those who have power can generalize and decree their group characteristics as representative of the national culture. With this decree, the dominant group necessarily depreciates all characteristics belonging to subordinate groups, characteristics that deviate from the decreed patterns" (P. Freire & Macedo, 1987, p. 52). Although egregious, the law is the flashpoint for other inequities noted by the authors, including access to appropriately trained teachers, opportunities for teacher professional development for working with ELLs, appropriate assessments to measure achievement among ELLs, instructional time to accomplish learning goals, instructional materials and curriculum, adequate facilities, and intense segregation in low-performing schools.

Laws and Critical Language and Literacy

Prendergast (2002) employs CRT in her review of the intersections of race, literacy, and federal law. She offers a legal timeline to consider connections between racial polices and literacy, examines primary source documents, critiques legal arguments, includes biographies of the major stakeholders, deconstructs sociohistorical contexts, and illustrates "cultural biases that seem to inform their approach to literacy" (p. 211). She explains how the U.S. Supreme Court adopted a framework that acknowledged Whiteness and literacy as the property of Whites by examining several pivotal U.S. Supreme Court cases. Prendergast claims that, in each case, the Court's view of Whiteness as property underpinned its decision regarding educational equity for African Americans. She draws upon CLS and CRT to critique the way that race has been situated in education, alleging that legislation has failed to recognize the importance of equal education for African Americans as a noteworthy enterprise in a democratic society. She believes that the reccurring idea of a national "literacy crisis" is a blind that has stalled the civil rights movement and the improvement of living conditions for African Americans.

Prendergast submits that part of the argument that is not taken up by CRT in reviewing these court cases is worth consideration—how literacy has played a significant role in what Whites think about education's worth, and, by extension, how literacy is maintained as the property of Whites. She examines the role of race and literacy in *Washington v. Davis*, pointing out that the Court held a restricted definition of literacy that was bound to the ability to quantify literacy performance: "the abilities to read, write, and memorize are highly contextual and task dependent with limited transferability to new contexts and tasks, and hence it is not possible to speak of a single, normative literacy" (p. 217). She argues that the Court's "common sense" use of the term *literacy* appeared to be aligned with the alleged "literacy crisis" in the nation and the conception of literacy as White property. Likewise, in the *Bakke* case, she observes that "the standards used to judge literacy attainment as racially and culturally neutral—standards whose arbitrary nature had not been examined even in the face of a racially disparate impact" were at stake (p. 223). Prendergast argues that, historically, Whites have worked to position literacy as neutral, acultural, and racially indeterminate, and to depict low literacy rates as the result of individual, familial, or racial failures.

Gutiérrez (2001) also examines federal court cases and follow-up laws that address the nexus of race, class, immigrant status, and language in the United States. She argues that although the Bilingual Education Act and Title I programs exist, they are operationalized within narrow ideological frameworks that marginalize (if not demonize) students who do not exemplify the American standard: White, middle-class, and English-dominant. She observes that current federal laws emphasize a "one-size-fits-all" standard, while Underserved students are simultaneously being taught by many un/underprepared teachers. She declares that language "has become the new proxy for race in both public and educational policies. Refining the categories of difference makes it easier to identify and subsequently 'socialize' linguistically different students" (p. 566). Gutiérrez writes that students' identities as bi/multicultural and bi/multilinguistic individuals are being shortchanged by current research, instruction, policies, and laws that control and enforce a normalizing view of language.

Anne Haas Dyson (2003a) examines the notion of "all" children that was used in national campaigns to win support of the NCLB Act, as well as subsequent narrow definitions of literacy research that have been used by the federal government and restrictions that have been placed on state and local school districts seeking federal funds. She argues that *all* is a euphemism for children who are "not middle class and not white" (p. 100). She believes that under these circumstances, *all* is part of an ideological stance—what she calls the "nothing assumption"—where the children most in need of support are portrayed as bringing nothing of value or worth to literacy learning. Dyson advocates for greater teacher learning and training to recognize, appreciate, and build upon the multiple frames of knowledge, texts, and meaning systems that different children bring to school.

Olivos and de Valladolid's (2005) review of federal (Elementary and Secondary Education Act of 1965, Title VII, replaced as Title III under the 2003 No Child Left Behind Act) and state laws (California Propositions 187, 209, and 227) outlines their influence on Latina/o and bilingual education. They argue that the federal law "reaffirms the traditional federal view of ELLs as deficient and thus in need of compensatory education programs to overcome their deficiencies. . . . NCLB favors English-only instruction or alternative English language acquisition programs over bilingual education programs" (p. 289). A lynchpin of NCLB is accountability; it is a system built based on meritocracy, whereby standards support the status quo and normalize Whiteness.

The authors recall the effects of several California propositions and suggest that policymakers who are fearful of the population shift have crafted law as a "manipulation of the provision or the exclusion of educational opportunities for our students and other students of Color" (p. 285). They use discourse analysis to explicate how those in power use language to describe "nondominant languages, particularly Spanish, as problematic to the cohesiveness of the country [and] the success of Latino students" (p. 286). Their analysis centers on demystifying the achievement gap between Anglos and Spanish speakers and revealing how the focus on the gap in test scores tends to "obfuscate the glaring inequities found in our public school system and in society that preclude the authentic participation and integration of communities of Color into 'mainstream' society" (p. 286). They argue that the use of generic, homogeneous identifiers hides individual differences among students of Color, especially in the Latino community, where students may differ by nation of origin, immigration status, and class. The authors note a discourse where language and other oppressions intersect (race, class, immigration) but are ignored. They also clarify that social inequalities are in greater need of change than is the focus on language as the single determiner of achievement gap differences.

Religion

In the West, religion is separated from broader notions of spirituality and is understood as a formalized or sanctioned religion (animism, Buddhism, Christianity, Hinduism, Islam, and Judaism). Although a part of CT (Wiggershaus, 2006), religion has remained distant from critical theories. Worldwide religious oppression is fraught with overtones of mass murders and genocide that occur as powerful nations or groups seek to eradicate the religious beliefs of others.

Abu El-Haj (2002) and Re'em (2001) interrogate the intersections of politics, race, and religion in language use during the post-9/11 era for Muslim and Arab immigrant youth and the sanctioning of Christianity as Eurocentric, respectively. Pennycook and Coutand-Marin (2003) also focus on how language is used to encourage the teaching of English, especially among the poor and people of Color, as part of the messianic call to spread Christianity. They review advertisements and recruitment materials that promote the teaching of English as a ministry. They conclude that these materials strongly support conservative, right-wing, narrowly defined understandings of Christian and evangelical ideology, which are politically linked to the economic and capitalist regime of the United States.

Baquedano-Lopez (2004) examines the intersection of race, class, and language within the power structures of a community and the Catholic church, or what she calls the "official and unofficial institutional practices" (p. 214). This study focuses on the local politics that informed a shift from a Saturday-morning religious education program in both English and Spanish to English only. The Spanish program (*doctrina*) was designed for first-generation Spanish-speaking immigrant children (mostly from Mexico, but also from Argentina, El Salvador, and Peru) in a parish in Los Angeles. Using ethnographic techniques and discourse analysis, Baquedano-Lopez (2004) examines documents that represent "the official voices of the parish" (p. 213). She finds that the shift in policy reflects deeper issues in the nation and state regarding immigrant status, education, and language debates.

Economics and Critical Consciousnesses

Taxel (2002) offers an example in his analyses of the "fast capitalism" that drives the publication of children's literature. Adopting neo-Marxist and critical cultural studies stances, he critiques the ideological hegemony that is shaping children's literature and driving multinational publishing conglomerates, including, but not limited to, the publication and use of multicultural children's literature. He explains publication trends that appeal to largely White audiences, from classics to popular culture. Taxel also reveals that industry claims of multicultural literature include non-English editions, non-White characters, and folklore and animal substitutes for people. He notes serious concerns among cultural insiders and the publishing industry about what constitutes cultural authenticity and for whom multicultural books are written. In sum, Taxel calls on publishers and editors to resist economic pressures, and he promotes the use of quality children's literature to teach children how to read critically and multiculturally.

A. Luke (2004) seeks to assess education in our global market economy through a sweeping analysis of reform efforts that have occurred in Australia, Canada, New Zealand, the United Kingdom, and the United States. He observes a systematic, orchestrated, and concerted effort on the part of right-wing politicians to dominate, surveil, define, and narrowly structure the profession of teacher education from educating to credentialing teachers. He also suggests that teachers under these systems of domination can become cookie-cutter ideologues who retain their jobs as long as they work within federal and state mandates: "The U.S. federal government tied Title I funding to the use of scientifically proven curriculum materials in No Child Left Behind. This has amounted to a de facto endorsement of Open Court Readers and other phonics-based reading series nationally" (p. 1433). He foresees other English-dominant countries following suit with nationally endorsed readers and materials. He calls for teacher reeducation that acknowledges how publishers have expanded beyond textbooks to include more multimedia materials, making literacy a commodity.

Meadmore and Meadmore (2004) review the marketing strategies used by 30 private, elite Australian schools and link the schools' efforts to corporate models, government images of public schooling, and religious appeals. Their window of comparison consists of schools in Australia, New Zealand, the United Kingdom, and the United States. They observe that the materials are promoted as a way to obtain educational excellence, where "accountability, efficiency, and effectiveness are indicators and measures of achievement" (p. 376). In what they call the "purchasing of education" (p. 378), promotions and advertisements push "the intrinsic value of a superior education" (p. 378). Collectively, the promotions contain three over-powering themes: (1) the value of education for life and self-esteem, (2) emotional intelligence and skills, and (3) religious principles.

Lucey and Reay (2002) also study the marketization of education at British secondary schools, linking perceptions of select schools to government-published reports, media evaluations, parental viewpoints, and student narratives. They suggest that there is a firm perception of failing schools and "fantasized" schools (p. 260). Failing schools and students are demonized as "deviant, criminal, and violent." It is implied that "pupils were stupid; that 'too many' ethnic minority pupils attended; that teachers were lax and uncaring" (p. 254). Official government documents and student narratives also criticize schools that educate working-class students, noting that they hold little social status and are marked by gender, linguistic, and racial/ethnic differences, and low academic achievement. Fantasized schools and students are glorified as "perfect," desirable, without violence, holding social status, unmarked by gender and racial/ethnic differences, and academically high-achieving. A common assumption is that students who attend the demonized schools will not attain social, economic, personal, or professional satisfaction in their lives, while those who attend the fantasized schools are nearly assured such sucess (Lucey & Reay, 2002).

Brandt (2003) also believes that literacy is an economic asset. Her research includes interviews with "average Americans" over a 5-year period as she sought to better understand how literacy has changed throughout their lives and to predict how it may change in the near future:

> Seeing who was sponsoring whose literacy, how, for what, and to what degree made it possible to apprehend deeper causes for literacy inequity—the stratified systems of sponsorship stretching far beyond individual families and schools that affect access to, achievement of, and reward for literacy. (p. 247)

She challenges current misunderstandings of the Black/White achievement gap that point to individual, familial, or community failings yet fail to address historical, political, social, and economic abuse of power and status as exposed through the literate lives of her interviewees.

Many of the political and economic forces that are part of the structural domain of power also affect the funding and publication of critical language and literacy research. It is a threat to First Amendment rights when funding agencies and publication power elites deny funding for publications that challenge conservative views, federal legislation, and "American values."

Disciplinary Domain of Power

Collins's (2000) disciplinary domain of power notes that oppression is "a way of ruling that relies on bureaucratic hierarchies and techniques of surveillance" (p. 298). In this domain, oppression is maintained "through the ways in which organizations are run" (p. 280). For instance, bureaucratic rules, regulations, protocols, policies, and practices support existing power structures by "reproducing intersecting oppressions and . . . masking their effects" with rhetoric about the import of competence, reasonableness, and equality (p. 281).

Critical Consciousness Within Indigenous Schools and Communities

Language is the conduit for many sources of knowing. McCarty et al. (2005) contend that "local knowledges and ways of knowing are encoded in and expressed through local languages, language is central to any discussion of Indigenous epistemologies, education, and human rights" (p. 2). Language and literacy express cultural knowledge and meaning systems, as mirrored in the work of Indigenous scholars and their allies [see, for instance, Harrison and Papa's (2005) Maori-language immersion school among the Waikato-Tainui in New Zealand and Kawakami and Dudoit's (2000) Native Hawaiian language immersion program in Hilo].

By contrast, Kaomea (2005) critiques the sanctioned histories and interpretations of Native Hawaiians' epistemology, culture, and language and the images used to teach Hawaiian studies in elementary textbooks. She maintains that an Indigenous studies curriculum taught discourses that "legitimize past colonial oppressions of the Hawaiian people [and] create a fear or distrust of current movements toward Hawaiian self-determination" (p. 29). Her review of student work documents how these discourses, textbooks, and forms of instruction reinforce Western European and Asian superiority by demonizing Native Hawaiian religious and cultural practices and painting stereotypical, unflattering, and inaccurate descriptions of the past.

She also observes a growing trend by Japanese American scholars to re-envision their role in the colonial history of Hawai'i and dismiss "their personal and collective complicity in the continued oppression of Indigenous Hawaiians"(p. 38). Further, she argues that teachers need to "question how they may be wittingly or unwittingly serving as collaborators in the perpetuation of Hawai'i's hegemonic dynamics" (p. 38). Kaomea finds that non-Hawaiian classroom teachers resist and misuse the curriculum and reproduce images of Hawaiian savagery and infanticide that were promoted during colonization, which may help prevent Native Hawaiians from reaching their goal of land sovereignty.

Indigenous scholars also believe that connections between sovereignty and self-determination bind epistemologies, culture, and language together. Lomawaima and McCarty (2002) succinctly articulate that "contradictions in federal Indian education policy can be understood as attempts by the government to determine which aspects of Indian life are 'safe' and allowable and which are so radically different that they are perceived as dangerous to the nation-state" (p. 283). The contradictions present two coexistent beliefs: (1) Native people's commitment to self-determination, and (2) multiple tactics by the government to halt such commitment.

Navajo scholar Manuelito (2005) chronicles federal policies toward Indians that have been used to justify injustice, colonialism, and suffering in her community as part of the Indian Self-Determination Act and Educational Assistance of 1975. She writes that federal policies "can be annulled at any time by congressional action," which is an abusive use of power (p. 73). Her commentary foreshadows a discussion of the hope that Native peoples have in policies to improve their formal education and help them realize levels of academic self-determination. Manuelito examines how self-determination was carried out in the community-controlled Ramah Navajo School. She recounts the displacement and resistance of the Ramah Navajo throughout the community's history with White settlers and federal legislation, including a discussion of forced residential schools that were established to destroy Navajo language and culture. She believes that the Ramah Navajo School's successful battles in U.S. courts have had the greatest impact on framing the people's sense of self-determination, which is grounded in Navajo epistemology.

Suina (2004), who is a Cochiti Pueblo, examines the approach taken by teachers in addressing Indigenous language and culture. He describes the language shift from the oral cultures of the Pueblo Indians and shows how Native language teachers are helping students retain and maintain the many languages that are spoken by New

Mexico Pueblo Indians. Drawing on interviews and the personal life stories of six Pueblo Indians, Sunia shares their "unqualified dedication to the language and culture of their people," despite the onslaught of "school-based cultural and linguistic genocide practices" (pp. 289, 298). He concludes the importance of "Pueblo-specific" instruction by offering examples of changes that teachers have made to strengthen Native language use and culture (p. 300). Likewise, Arapaho scholar Marker (2000) claims, "If researchers wish to engage in a genuine praxis with tribal people they must first acknowledge the local structure of critical narratives about schooling. Aboriginal people have an identity that is profoundly connected to a sense of place . . . that distinguishes them from other minorities" (p. 412).

Ball (2004) examines a Canadian program among First Nations communities that helps support cultural and linguistic heritages. She acknowledges Canada's history of genocide and colonialism and the suffering of First Nations people, especially in regard to language and cultural loss and forced residential schooling. Indigenous knowledge, research, and theory and the practices of the West work together in a new program, which is sanctioned by the Elders and is respectfully "grounded in the worldviews, beliefs, and norms of those who conceptualize and teach the curricula" (p. 456). Ball reveals how the Generative Curriculum Model includes First Nations and Eurocentric ideas that are focused on "uncovering new, community-relevant knowledge sources, considering knowledge that resides in communities and creating fresh understandings from reflection and dialogue" (p. 460) where lessons are planned and taught collaboratively.

Jiménez, Smith, and Martinez-León (2003) also recognize the importance of Indigenous languages in their study of language and literacy practices in central Mexico, which are informed by postcolonial and neocolonial understandings of European Spanish and Mexican Spanish, as well as current influences from France and the United States. They describe how linguistic domination arose as "the colonial experience served to create a historically conditioned context in which not only native literacies were prohibited but also Mexicans' use of the colonizers' language and literacy became defined as perennially deficient" (p. 492), or what they call "*layered colonialism*" (p. 493, emphasis in original). Mexican Spanish was imposed upon the Indigenous people, creating a linguistic domination or linguistic cultural capital where "forms of language can be translated into social and economic advantage in a 'linguistic marketplace'" (p. 493). They argue that European colonization has led to linguistic domination and the reproduction of language, ideas, and procedures that help sustain Europe's domination.

Jiménez and colleagues examine the ideological hegemony underlying Mexico's literacy policies and school instruction. They articulate their understandings through in-depth descriptions of the languages and literacies used in the community, and the types of schools, teachers, and instruction. Their study was conducted in two primary and two elementary classrooms, and it included community literacy. They describe the language of the largest ethnic people (Nahua) in their setting, whose Indigenous language is Nahatal, while noting that Spanish is the language used in schools and community. In schools and communities, they explore how language and literacy were used to "document activities and behaviors that most often go unnoticed because of their ordinariness," thereby revealing differences and effects on students and teachers (p. 491).

Results of their analysis within schools reveal restrictive language and literacy practices that focused on penmanship, where students were quickly corrected and prohibited from using colloquialisms in writing. Instruction in oral reading mirrored that of school writing, being very formal and restrictive. By way of contrast, community members expressed themselves freely in written language, nearly invisibly, which prompted the researchers to suggest that "at least one of the purposes of publicly displayed texts is to allow a more democratic medium for communication between those who are marginalized through dominant literacy practices" (p. 502).

Importantly, the authors (university researchers and graduate students) reveal their country of birth, language proficiencies, and understandings of both Mexican culture both in general and the culture within the study's specific geographic area. Although all are fluent and proficient Spanish speakers and have lived in Mexico at different periods in their lives, none of the principal researchers was a Mexican national or native Spanish speaker. Several of the graduate students were, however, and their insights of cultural and linguistic knowledge were added to the analysis of the data. The inclusion of this information is paramount, for it acknowledges that although every researcher was a fluent Spanish speaker, each one spoke Spanish differently, depending on where he or she learned Spanish and how often he or she used Spanish, debunking ideas of monolithic Spanish language and discourse. Further, the researchers' varied Spanish-language backgrounds and language proficiencies suggest that linguistic knowledge and proficiency were not enough to give them entrée into the community or knowledge of the culture. Finally, this study offers invaluable insights because the researchers worked in collaborative and mutually informing relationships with one another and with the members of the community.

In another study of community, Kalman (2000) presents the work of "public scribes who are known as typists or *mecanógrafos*" in Mexico City (p. 188). She tracks how *mecanógrafos* learned their trade and the cultural role and collaborative nature of literacy that these scribes offer—from completing required government documents to homework. She views their role in society as "functioning as written language broker." They "allow clients to take part in those social situations that require the use of writing, situations in which they might otherwise not be able to participate" (p. 188). Participating *mecanógrafos* had several years of formal schooling and learned their trade from a variety of sources (observation, questioning, practice, copying, clients, and so forth). They demonstrate the complexity of the literate world that is encountered daily by *mecanógrafos* who seek to address the needs of each client.

Language, Literacy, and Culture

Much of the research within the disciplinary domain of power focuses on language use and reform among users of non-English languages or heritage languages. The importance of the intersection of language, literacy, and culture should not be overlooked, as Hall (1982) emphasizes:

> Language is the medium *par excellence* through which things are "represented" in thought and thus the medium in which ideology is generated and transformed. But in language, the same social relation can be differently represented and construed. (pp. 36–37, italics in original)

For instance, Olivo (2003) describes the conflict that arises between theories of English as a Second Language (ESL) instruction and the reality of classroom instruction in one Canadian school, where ESL students are often "subjected to institutional control in the classroom in ways that constrain their ability to practice, and, thus, learn English, the dominant language" (p. 50). He contends that classroom teachers' ideologies frame their interactions with ESL students, and result in direct, authoritative, controlling behaviors that delimit access to language practice. Of particular import are teacher behaviors (he labels these "official" classroom interactions) that consist of turn-taking and speaking/talking lessons that can hinder English acquisition. Further, he suggests that they are "possible means by which the unequal relations between minority and majority ethnic and linguistic groups are reproduced in the school setting" (p. 67). Olivo recommends interactions that promote student talk to improve language acquisition and development in the classroom.

Meador (2005) uses a critical anthropological lens to examine the acculturation of Mexican immigrant girls into small rural communities in the Southwest that have a history of "noncompliance with Title VI of the Civil Rights Act, which guarantees special assistance to ELLs" (p. 151). Her explanation of White flight is helpful in understanding attitudes within the community and school toward Mexican immigrants as ELL. Meador's research, conducted in two different middle schools, records different approaches to addressing ELLs' similar regimes for the placement of students in ESL programs, and comparable sociocultural perspectives about what it means to be "good students." She documents that initial placement is often predicated on an informal conversation with the ESL teacher whose recommendation places students in or out of services after the first meeting, which violates current law. In this context, a "good student," whether the student is male or female, excels athletically, academically, and socially as "institutionalized by the daily practices of grading and ability grouping within classrooms" (p. 157). This cultural norm placed Mexicanas at a severe disadvantage, where their intersecting oppressions (class, gender, language, immigrant status, and race/ethnicity) worked against their ability to excel. When queried about Mexicanas, teachers described them as "low achievement, low motivation, and low status " (pp. 154–155), with little regard to how language growth affected areas of social growth. Meador believes "the hegemonic ideology that measures academic performance in terms of English proficiency and participation in school sports is rooted in the small-town definition of what it means to be American" (p. 161). Further, she argues that the use of English is considered a sign of being "American"—a trend that reinforces and resegregates U.S. schools. When communities, administrators, and teachers adopt this concept, it also reproduces the inequities within society.

Critical language and literacy scholars encourage all teachers to develop multilingual classrooms where heritage and home languages are welcomed. Linguistic support is not limited to foreign languages but includes variations of English (L. Green, 2002; Wheeler & Swords,

2004) and classrooms where multiple languages are spoken (Rymes & Anderson, 2004). Delpit (2002) observes that African American English is not valued in schools or society and that we must struggle for it to be recognized as a legitimate language within "the educational power structure" (p. xviii). Similarly, Alim's (2005) analysis of Black Language (BL) addresses the way BL is depicted in federal courts and within the field of language and literacy research. He observes that some federal judges have recognized the importance of acknowledging and building on the social, cultural, and psychological nature of language; however, many language and literacy researchers appear resistant to address these issues. He recalls, for example, that the success of dialect readers to improve the reading achievement of Black students was based on a recognition and appreciation of linguistic, cultural, and social knowledges of the students' lives. Alim describes the Linguistic Profiling Project (LPP) at Stanford University as an example of a program that seeks to address many historic and current inequalities of language education and to teach "linguistically profiled and marginalized students about how language is used, and importantly, how language can be used against them" (p. 28). His critical and activist approach builds on the tremendous amount of underused linguistic research to addresses the intersections of race, class, and language.

Rogers (2002a) examines the process, narratives/scripts, and negotiations with power as experienced by one African American woman and her daughter. Rogers reveals how the notion of disability is socially constructed through discourse, as school officials use legal, technical, and educational language to their advantage. She also shows how a mother, who wants the best for her daughter, accepts the school officials' recommendations. The process and evidence used by school officials appear to confirm what Rogers calls "the 'discourse of deficits' . . . representing what children cannot do rather than what they can do" (p. 232). The procedures for moving this student into special education reproduced social inequities within the school system and the lives of the participants.

Theory into Practice

A number of studies focus on informal institutional policies and practices that highlight counternarratives about academic achievement among students of Color. Gayles (2005) points to the resilience exhibited by three high-school-aged African American males as they negotiated their intellectual prowess in an underresourced school without sacrificing their personal identities and without paying a heavy social cost. Lopez (2002) examines the disproportionate number of women who graduate from high school compared with their male peers in a predominantly second-generation Dominican New York City public school. She considers the intersectionality of oppression in response to three key questions: "How do formal and informal institutional practices within high schools 'race' and 'gender' students? How do racializ(ing) and gender(ing) processes intersect in the classroom setting? How can teachers work toward dismantling race, gender, and class oppression in their classrooms?" (p. 1188). She observes, for example, that the school's strong presence of security (male security guards) often profiled males as delinquent, which is reflective of a "discourse that links dark-skinned male bodies to crime and simultaneously attempts reallocate resources based on that definition" (p. 1193). Similarly, a discourse of criminality was attached to Black and Latino males, and it surfaced in classroom instruction.

In a focal classroom, a dedicated, albeit authoritarian, teacher used sarcasm, dismissive commentary, and public humiliation to gain control. The teacher strictly enforced formal rules (which were posted on the board) and informal rules (English only), and appeared more punitive toward males. Her efforts contrast with those of a teacher whose approach was transformative, where the formal and informal rules welcomed students' cultures, lived experiences, and languages. Lopez recommends that teachers "work toward ending race, gender, and class oppression by actively seeking to create a school climate that provides a space for the democratic discussion of racial, class, and gender inequality" (p. 1200).

Weis and Fine (2001) address issues of race, class, gender, and sexuality as they invite different groups of public middle and high school students as well as adults to engage in conversations that "deliberately and directly challenge inequity" (p. 498). Their participants were youth from privileged and poverty lifeworlds and adults who are committed to working for positive social change and a just society. They submit that "We must engage in the creation and production of 'counterpublics'—spaces where adults and youth can challenge the very exclusionary practices currently existing in public institutions—practices that inscribe inequalities by social class, race, gender, and sexuality" (p. 499). They describe two projects: one that addressed the production of a safe space within a public school to address class, race, ethnic, and gender inequalities, and another that examined how critical pedagogy supported positive social consciousness and community.

The first project, Womanfocus, guided by a Latina community aide, addresses sexuality in a racially and ethnically mixed middle school, a safe space where girls could share personal narratives, debunk stereotypes, and reshape their identities. Weis and Fine suggest that the counterpublic space helps the girls work "across race and ethnic lines in the group, thus rewriting dominant race scripts of difference in poor areas" (p. 505). The presence of this project in a public school disrupts traditional rules, policies, and practices of school-appropriate conversations, teacher-student interactions, and guidance.

The second project occurs in a racially and ethnically diverse, detracked public high school's world literature class. Students delve into the etymology of their names, concepts of ableness depicted in selected literature, and teachers' use of scaffolding for transformative thinking. To create a safe space, teachers aimed at "breaking down the invisible walls that segregate those historically privileged from those historically silenced" (p. 513). As more literature reflected the lives and experiences of writers of Color, White students began to embrace their Whiteness as cultural capital, bonding around their Whiteness, social class, status, or experiences when their ideas were challenged by students of Color. This project created tensions within the community, as the researchers and classroom teachers sought to break the stranglehold on the reproduction of social inequality by creating more equitable and democratic spaces for learning.

Similarly, Duncan (2002a) conducted observations and interviews of African American male high school students, teachers, and administrators in an examination of the marginalization of African American males. He sought to acknowledge and celebrate the voices of African American males, who are so often maligned, characterized, and pathologized as "beyond love" (p. 131). He used the lens of CRT because it "privileges the narratives of those who have been victimized to ameliorate the conditions attendant to oppression and domination and, in particular, engages the problem . . . in ways [that] generate new social theories in the service of liberation" (p. 141). His counternarratives are powerful antidotes to traditional imperceptive academic descriptions of the racial/ethnic epistemologies used by African American males to read/write their world. He recommends allowing and accepting the knowledges, languages, and voices of Black males in order to encourage them to navigate among and within home, community, and school contexts and to give them a place to start reforming their education.

Summary

The current movement in criticality is reflected in the critical theorizing and research of language and literacy. We review and critique research categorized within Collins's (1990, 2000) structural and disciplinary domains of power. These studies trace the historical presence of language use in federal legislation, state law, curriculum requirements, textbooks, classroom discourse, and alternative programs. The descriptions of legal, and legally sanctioned, definitions of language and literacy continue to narrowly define these terms within the U.S. judicial and legislative branches of government, leaving personal agency unaccounted for. We call for additional critical reviews of how federally funded research, that is, literacy grants, are written as if they are ideologically, racially, culturally, and linguistically neutral in an acknowledged diverse society.

There has been a noticeable shift in pronouncements of criticality among researchers—from passive opposition to ideological hegemony to activist declarations. Although a wide range of methodologies, methods, and techniques are being used, a more limited range of critical theorizing is drawn upon for analyses. For many criticalists, especially scholars of Color, the demarcation between the political and personal is blurred. We recommend reconceptualizing language and literacy research to more explicitly address intersecting oppressions (class, gender, language, immigrant status, and race/ethnicity).

We found that premier language and literacy journals seldom include critical research that interrogates or challenges the structural and disciplinary domains that sustain power and inhibit social justice. This phenomenon suggests resistance within the field to embracing criticalist viewpoints. Several questions in language and literacy research arise that need to be addressed: How does the research context, both historically and currently, influence and inform questions and methods? How do prevailing ideological assumptions shape the terrain? How are the cultures, knowledges, languages, and social realities of participants part of the research process, including question formation, decision making, data collection, interpretation, analysis, and presentation of research? If Whiteness and sanctioned forms of Whiteness in language and literacy policies and practices are forms of White property, how do researchers reconcile race/ethnicity in studies that engage participants of Color, and bi/multilingual groups? The ideological hegemony that supports the continued mischaracterization of language and literacy is the focus of the next chapter.

CHAPTER 6

Critically Conscious Language and Literacy Research: Hegemonic Domain of Power

*But let justice roll down as waters, and righteousness
as a mighty stream.*
—Amos 5:24

We continue to use Collins's (1990, 2000) model within this chapter to review and critique critical language and literacy research that tackles the hegemonic domain of power as well as inherent domain levels. Collins defines the *hegemonic domain of power* as "a form or mode of social organization that uses ideas and ideology to absorb and thereby depoliticize oppressed groups' dissent" (p. 299). Key features within this domain are the development of critical consciousness to detect and dismantle the dominant ideologies, the construction of new knowledge, the commitment to the integrity of individuals, and the acknowledgment of freedom beyond existing parameters. Collins argues that "the significance of the hegemonic domain of power lies in its ability to shape consciousness via the manipulation of ideas, images, symbols, and ideologies" (p. 285). Importantly, the domain accepts that counter-hegemonic knowledge exists and is used to shape consciousness (Collins, 2000). Language and literacy research often fails to acknowledge that "there can be no disinterested, objective, and value-free definition of literacy: The way literacy is viewed and taught is always and inevitably ideological" (Auerbach, 1991, p. 71). To that end, researchers have sought to define *critical literacy* and *critical pedagogy*.

Defining Critically Conscious
Language and Literacy Research

Beck (2005) writes that critical literacy "places in the foreground issues of power and explicitly attends to differences across race, class, gender, sexual orientation and so on" (p. 393). Hefferman and Lewison (2005) contend that critical literacy is "where literacy is viewed as an avenue for developing social viewpoints and interrogating social norms" (p. 108). They note that it is important because "the literacy learned in school rarely leads to an understanding of how language and social systems work to empower or disempower people" (p. 108). Leland, Harste, and Huber (2005) draw from the work of A. Luke and Freebody (1997) as they posit that critical literacy "includes a focus on social justice and the role that each of us plays in challenging or helping to perpetuate the injustices we identify in our world" (p. 259). Rogers (2002c) characterizes critical literacy as "an interactive process dependent on the (local) interactions between the teacher and the student and the texts and curriculum (institutional), as well as on the discourses that are being discussed and critiqued (societal)" (p. 784). Morrell (2005) defines *critical literacies* as "literacies involving the consumption, production, and distribution of print and new media texts by, with, and on behalf of marginalized populations in the interests of naming, exposing, and destabilizing power relations; and promoting individual freedom and expression" (p. 314). The popularity and use of media among school-aged children, especially teenagers, has heightened the need to critically analyze their use and production of media.

Numerous critically conscious language and literacy studies include descriptions of the race/ethnicity and language/s of participants, but the majority are students of Color from poorly resourced communities and schools. The participants' ability to translate and transcend the ideological hegemony that permeates their communities and schools is seldom examined. In addition, researchers in such studies generally self-identify in limited confessional personal ways as White, middle-class, monolingual English, and female; they often fail to interrogate their privileged status. McIntyre (1997) explains: "white people's lack of consciousness about their racial identities limits their ability to critically examine their own positions as racial beings who are implicated in the existence and perpetuation of racism" (p. 16). Thompson (2003) also suggests that many Whites aim to "position ourselves as 'good whites.' . . . [W]e can acknowledge white racism as a generic fact, it is hard to acknowledge as a fact about ourselves" (p. 8). We submit that ideological hegemony influences the way studies have been conceived, conducted, analyzed, and interpreted.

Critically Conscious Studies Among White Students

There is a small but growing body of studies that address students' Whiteness and gender. Blair (2000) discusses gender and talk in a Canadian middle school classroom, where her idea of *genderlects* emerges. She finds that the discourse of boys and girls generally adheres to stereotypes of girls seeking private, small-group, soft-spoken spaces and boys seeking public, group, loud spaces, while dismissing the rude, racist, sexual, and homophobic language used by boys in the classroom. Although Blair's research is conducted in a multiracial/multiethnic setting, she does not adequately address how her notions of male and female discourse reflect White, European, middle-class values and normative values and beliefs about the superiority of Whiteness.

Hicks (2000) presents a study in which she worked both in and out of classrooms over a period of 18 months with a small group of 3rd- and 4th-grade girls. The girls in this study are assumed to be White because when race is not specifically mentioned, it is generally understood to be White. Hicks mentions that some of the girls in the class resembled the blonde-haired, blue-eyed girls in the novels they read. She also writes that the geographical locale of the study is Appalachia, among "working-poor whites" (Hicks, 2000, p. 64). She posits that concerns about language and identity are intimately tied to notions of social-class differences.

Hicks's focus on gender, language, pedagogy, and social class explicates differences between dominant middle-class values and literacy expectations and the values and expectations held by the study's participants. She uses literature that she believes contains themes that are relevant to the lives of her participants; however, participants appear to be fascinated by different narratives: scary stories, stories involving the dead or witchcraft, and stories that use a "cuss" word or two. Hicks (2000) views their preferences as being reflective of their Appalachian roots and their sense of powerlessness. She admits to having misinterpretations about what she thought would engage the girls in conversations about literature. Her lack of awareness, as she points out, reveals an evolving critical consciousness about Whiteness, poverty, and preadolescent girls. By way of comparison, the participants appear to be critically aware of their own lives (their poverty, culture, folkways, language, and the way the media popularizes the lives of girls whose lives are very different from their own). They also seem to be aware of the researcher's lack of cultural understanding, middle-classness, mainstream views of literature, expected responses, and power to shape the research experience through book selection, questioning, and prompts.

Several studies focus on the intersection of literacy, technology/ online outlets/sources, and the formation of social identities among English-dominant, upper- to upper-middle-class, adolescent White girls (Guzzetti & Gamboa, 2004, 2005; Merchant, 2001, 2005) and English-dominant, low- and middle-class White males and females (Lewis & Fabos, 2005). Each study encourages the literacy community to incorporate greater critical analysis of the literacy processes used in digital media and their effect on social identity formation. Gilyard (2000) proffers, without undermining the importance of research on broad notions of identity, "It's helpful at times to complicate notions of identity, but primary identities operate powerfully in the world and have to be productively engaged" (p. 270). He continues by admonishing researchers not to downplay the importance of interrogating what he calls "primary identities" or replacing them with notions of hybridity that too often lead to inaccurate and incomplete descriptions and characterizations of groups.

The relationship between the researcher and the participants' responses to literature is highlighted in a private homeschool setting where Young (2001) examines responses to literature with a focus on the identity and masculinity of four (White) young boys. She uses CDA to examine intersections among identity, masculinity, literacy, and social contexts. Young's (2000, 2001) work among White males reveals a gap in the literature—a paucity of critical literacy in the United States that focuses on White male students. Similarly, Hinchman, Payne-Bourcy, Thomas, and Olcott (2002) present a cross-study analysis that draws on data from larger studies of adolescent literacies, "where race and gender were not foregrounded" to look specifically at White males' interactions with literacy (p. 229). They constructed three case studies of White males' literacy to ascertain if issues of race, class, and gender were evident in their literacy practices. The findings reflect the foci of the original studies and reveal complex identities. The authors believe that identity should not be grounded in stereotypical notions of White male hegemony or bounded by simplistic notions of race, class, and gender.

Hinchman and Young's (2001) work among White students sought to uncover "some of the origins of inequity in literacy education" (p. 244). They also use CDA to re-examine data and to better understand the participation patterns of students in literacy classroom discussions. They describe the multiple and varied subjectivities of the students, but they do not engage issues of race, class, gender, and language as fully as one might expect, given the diversity of students in the classroom. From this work, they surmise that it is possible to use CDA to locate inequity in literacy education.

Concentrating on issues of power, Monahan (2003) examines language use aimed at raising the critical consciousness of 6th graders. In her study, students become detectives of "'local literacies,' or language varieties, . . . [which are no longer] merely exotic specialty items for the educated language consumer" (p. 207). Within her predominantly White student population, there are growing numbers of culturally and linguistically diverse students, which reflects economic and social changes that are occurring in the area. The students' study of language supported their evolving knowledge and understanding of how power is implicated in language wars: determining languages of power and privilege, and determining who is authorized to speak and on what issues. We are hopeful that CWS will serve as a model for future critically conscious language and literacy research.

Critically Conscious Studies of Sexual Orientation

The role of gender in language and literacy research is often described in the dichotomous language of male/female and boy/girl that Blackburn (2003) simultaneously abhors and uses. She approaches research from queer theory, critical feminism, CRT, and New Literacy Studies (NLS) perspectives in her examination of language and literacy among lesbian, gay, bisexual, transgender, and questioning (LGBTQ) youth in a community setting called The Loft. As a participant observer during the initial 3-year study, she observed and documented the youths' readings of the word and their worlds. Her focal participants were "visibly diverse" and self-identified as African American and African American–White biracial, from low-income socioeconomic circumstances (p. 467).

Blackburn (2003) seeks to support LGBTQ youth as they work against heterosexism, homophobia, and transphobia. She focuses on how a group of students used *literacy performance,* defined as "performances [in which] literacy has the opportunity to reinforce but also interrupt power dynamics. Integral to . . . [an] understanding of literacy performances is the agency of the readers and writers" (pp. 468–469).

The participants' struggle to address transphobia also reflects their consciousness of privilege, often understood as power over groups or individuals. Blackburn recognizes that the inequalities these youth face outside of The Loft are reinforced in some of their relations within The Loft because of the ways in which privilege and power are used by members within both small and large groups. She concludes that many of the youth have learned to work against oppression and hatred and to work for social change in the larger world while also working for change with their peers. She recommends that researchers "interrogate relationships between literacy performances and power dynamics in which we engage—not with the belief that we will ever achieve a perfectly just community or society, but with the understanding that the justice lies in the perpetual interrogation" (p. 498). She indicates that issues of class and race arise, but she does not interrogate them fully.

In 2005, Blackburn adopts the concept of borderland discourses to "reveal and make sense of the multiple meanings being conveyed and what difference these meanings make in the lives of those engaging in the discourse" (p. 96). She expands her research to include discussions of Gaybonics, a Black gay slang that combines notions of Ebonics and gay vocabulary. She believes the students created Gaybonics to help "liberate themselves in language, by making language inaccessible to their oppressors . . . eliciting pleasure among themselves and subverting homophobia and other forms of oppression including ageism and racism" (Blackburn, 2005, p. 91). As a participant observer, she worked collaboratively with her participants in analyzing and interpreting the data. The use of Gaybonics and the compiling of a Gaybonics dictionary included—as well as excluded—some of the gay youth at The Loft. This invited a conversation about Gaybonics and power, where non-Black gay youth felt alienated from the discourse and the project and Black gay youth took ownership over its use, refusing to publish the dictionary. Blackburn argues, "youth engaged in the Gaybonics in ways that constructed borders within their community to practice for other communities where they needed to construct such borders to protect themselves from the homophobia that they experienced . . . to subvert oppression" (p. 101). She finds that intimacy, mutual recognition, communication, resistance, and subversion within their multicontextual lives gave youth a sense of agency.

Blackburn (2003) self-identifies as a White woman and as "gay, lesbian, and queer" (pp. 472–473). Like some of her participants, she shifts her identity markers (always acknowledging each marker) depending on the community in which her identity is being shared. Although she claims to draw upon CRT in her theoretical discussions, it is not apparent in her work, which privileges sexual orientation. Too often, she glosses over notions of race and gender identity, suggesting that the tensions between these socially constructed concepts and queer and postmodern notions "work against the oppression that comes from being named, labeled, and tagged" (p. 472). The tensions among stances are best illustrated in her marginalization of the voices of girls of Color. Blackburn prefers to eliminate all identifiers and classifications because they oversimplify the complexity of people's identities, yet, in doing so, she privileges sexual orientation and subverts race and class in discussions of privilege and power among LGBTQ youth.

Carlson (2001) addresses homosexual identity, literacy, and dialogue using personal narrative. He historicizes how national, social, and political changes have affected language and identity and notes that "gayness" is portrayed stereotypically as "an upper-middle-class, white thing" (p. 298). His own understanding, consciousness, and comfort with terms used to sexually identify people, such as *queer*, has evolved overtime. Carlson draws on the notion of cyborg queer: "a metaphor for 'shapeshifting' subjects who exist at the boundaries and interfaces between outside and inside; between subjectivity, body, and technology; able to adapt to a heterogeneous and rapidly changing environment" (p. 305). After comparing and contrasting modernist and postmodernist views of identity, Carlson decides that the Internet offers a virtual community where identity can be revealed, concealed, imagined, and real. Carlson does not acknowledge that people of African descent were brought to this nation against their will and that their oppression was supported by systematic racism. We find this comparison of the oppression of African Americans and homosexuals troubling and uninformed. He likens gay life and experiences to the African American experience, erroneously coupling the histories, oppressions, and struggles experienced by African Americans in the United States with the history, oppression, and struggles experienced by homosexuals.

Linné (2003) suggests ways in which the media in general and technology in particular act as conduits that inform the identity formation of homosexuals. With a strong focus on literacy, he details how his online discussion group provides participants with a space to articulate their growing queer-consciousness and identity. He uses the term *proto-queers* to describe "individuals with queer feelings yet lacking the language to name them . . . left with personal desires that have no social context to give them meaning" (p. 670). Coming-out narratives, he argues, serve as an initial model for some, but too often, they are presented in an overly romanticized view "explaining the transformative power of literature and art in terms of only self-affirmation" (p. 670). His analysis and interpretation of discussions are presented as a binary between dominant scripts and counterscripts, where online discussions helped participants envisage themselves differently from the way they are projected in media and literature. He concludes, "Some participants saw queerness as the central component of their identities while others saw it more at the periphery, and some ethnic minorities did not feel entirely welcome in White-dominated gay culture" (pp. 671–672).

Critically Conscious Studies Among Students of Color

Nearly four-fifths of the critically conscious language and literacy research published between 2000 and 2005 includes reference to race, ethnicity, and identity. This reminds us of Hall's (2000) admonition that "Identity is not already 'there'; rather, it is a production, emergent, in process. It is situational—it shifts from context to context. . . . Its contradictions are negotiated, not 'resolved'" (p. xi). For instance, Lei (2003) examines the appropriateness of talk and gender, where Black girls are characterized as "loud" and Southeast Asian boys are characterized as "quiet." Specifically, Black girls are depicted as "unattractive within racist, sexist, and heterosexist discourses," and Southeast Asian males are depicted as quiet, mysterious, and simultaneously emasculated and ganglike (p. 168). Teachers and students use these stereotypical identity markers of the "Other" as "monolithic characterizations that homogenize diverse populations into subordinate racial groups" (p. 158). Both groups are perceived as a threat to the White male dominant power structure in the school. By contrast, Sumida (2000) describes and deconstructs the language and literacy of a Hawaiian 2nd-grade girl, noting her use of popular culture, Western notions of beauty and materialism, and gendered ideas about family and values. Unfortunately, Sumida's research is not informed by the scholarship of Native Hawaiian and Indigenous scholars to situate, understand, and interpret the child's text culturally.

Sutherland (2005) believes in "reading, writing and discussion as salient school literacy experiences through which students construct identities" (p. 371). She defines *identity* as "how an individual thinks about herself" (p. 369). She examines identity and blossoming notions of critical consciousness among Black adolescent girls as they transact with texts that are starting points for conversations as students share their daily, lived experiences and personal lives. Paramount to Sutherland is the way the young women interrogated the ascribed negative perceptions of their identity as Black young women and whether or not these perceptions became part of the boundaries of their identities. Her findings reveal that although the young women were aware of the negative stereotypes, they had more complex identities and understood their power to represent themselves in ways that were positive, healthy, and accurate.

Importantly, Sutherland, as a White woman, carefully acknowledges her position within historical, social, and interpersonal contexts. She trusts that her participants have been truthful with her, even though she is outside their lived realities. She accepts that White women can, and often do, separate race and gender, whereas African American women generally do not. Therefore, she sought out African American colleagues and read African American texts to better interpret her work. Sutherland's research supports the idea of culturally authentic literature for student identity formation, the importance of safe spaces to talk about literature with peers, and CRT's notion of language and literacy as conduits for producing counternarratives that reject racist, gendered, and class-based images of people of Color. Her ideas are consistent with those of Crenshaw (1997), who perceptively reveals that females of Color are "frequently constructed from the perspectives of those who are dominant within either the race or gender categories" (p. 112), implying that support from insiders is imperative.

By contrast, DeBlase (2003a, 2003b) examines the intersection of race, gender, and class among urban adolescent girls in a racially/ethnically diverse classroom. She seeks to understand how literacy transactions help to shape the girls' social identities by using their disengagement with classroom literacy—as well as their transactions with literature, personal stories, and discussions—as windows into their racial and social identities. DeBlase does not explicitly address issues of power, social injustice, or the history of injustice experienced by people of Color. In addition, she does not deconstruct the role of Whiteness and the lenses of femininity that she and the teacher brought to the classroom or the way the girls position and reposition issues of race, gender, and class as they transact with texts and interact with the teacher and researcher.

Martínez-Roldán (2003) examines the personal experiences and storytelling of a 2nd-grade bilingual Latina, informed by her understanding of storytelling as part of the rich cultural funds of knowledge that many Latino/a children bring to classrooms. She believes that classrooms where students are permitted to share their narratives in their first and second languages liberate the children and encourage linguistic and literacy growth. Martínez-Roldán thinks that, too often, mainstream teachers ignore or marginalize the culturally and linguistically rich lives of students who are not part of the mainstream, and thereby injure their academic identities.

Moje (2000) examines a diverse group of adolescent students of Color (Laotian, Latina/o, Samoan, and Vietnamese) who wish to align themselves with a "gangsta" lifestyle. Using CDA, she focuses on the students' use of language and literacy to express their aspirations and dramatize their fledgling understandings of "gangsta" discourse in multiple communicative ways. Despite their yearnings, the youth are not part of the gangsta life to which they aspire (in contradiction to the article's title). Their language and literacy use indicates a willingness to engage ideations of a gangsta lifestyle and reveals aspects of evolving identities. From her observations, Moje notes that "marginalized, gang-connected adolescents use literacy not only to resist, but also to make meaning about the events in their everyday lives" (p. 654). Moje observes students engaged in unsanctioned literacies that were far more sophisticated and complex forms of literacy than she had imagined, including "poetry, narrative, journal writing, letter writing, and novel reading" (p. 661). Moje's research raises a caution, as researchers excessively use the term *we* to characterize personal knowledges, or the field's presumed knowledges. Another approach is to localize what is known and by whom. Doing otherwise repositions all researchers as part of the dominant group. As Lamphere (1994) suggests, it is important to "interrogate the shifting boundaries of these identities and the ways they are implicated in social interaction and in how the structure of our educational institutions [serve] to move us back to the old set of assumptions" (p. 219).

Recently, Moje, Ciechanowski, Kramer, Ellis, Carrillo, and Collazo (2004) examined and located third space among the funds of knowledge students possess and the academic knowledges required in school literacy. Their study was conducted in Detroit among bilingual (Spanish-dominant) adolescents who identified themselves as Latino/a and came from many different home countries, yet resided in the United States. They argue that "content area learning suggests that the distance between everyday and academic Discourse is not as fast or immutable as one might believe" (p. 65). While recognizing, adopting, and adapting multiple funds of knowledge is necessary for the oppressed in a racist, classist, and homophobic society, the mis-use of funds of knowledge can be equally harmful. The authors con-clude that the participants drew upon multiple funds of knowledge to transverse their home and school spaces: "their identities potentially become hybrid because they are framed by a complex intersection of many different funds of knowledge and Discourses" (p. 69). They advocate the use of funds of knowledge, presence of third space, and hybrid Discourse as supportive tools upon which teachers can draw to improve the literacy performance of students, especially students of Color.

Members of this large and fluid research team possessed vary-ing levels of proficiency in Spanish, and all were English speakers. The multi-racial, multi-lingual research team expressed an awareness that their life experiences and socially constructed identity markers informed their methodology and data analyses. Pairs of English- and Spanish-dominant researchers, for example, conducted out-of-school interviews where the English-dominant speakers recognized codeswitching, but there was no reference to the importance of the insider knowledge/use of varying dialects of Spanish and how helpful this unrecognized knowledge was to the research project.

Not surprisingly, the researchers claim a very special relationship with the study's participants: "We have worked diligently to establish a sense of trust with these youth and their families, and the open-ness with which they share their experiences with us suggests that we have succeeded at some level" (p. 47). A student in this study cap-tures the position of many participants of Color when she asks, "Who do *you* think I am?" (p. 47, italics in the original). Her query suggests that she was cognizant of the researchers as White, and that the fact of Whiteness brings with it many unearned privileges. Moje et al., however, argue that student responses to queries about the research team's Whiteness suggest that the participants considered more than "phenotype and background" (p. 48). The students may have under-stood more about Whiteness than the researchers gave them credit for. From reading the world around them, the students were adept at knowing how and when they needed to adjust their interactions. For example, the researchers acknowledge that participants "displayed knowledge of *when* to say, do, or write certain information and they know *how* to say, do, or write such information" (p. 65, italics in the original). Collins (2003) has argued that "our ability to survive in hostile settings has hinged on our ability to learn intricate details about the behavior and world view of the powerful and adjust our behavior accordingly" (pp. 342–343). We submit that researcher advocacy must be informed by an understanding of the work of cultural insiders as well as personal quests. Brodkey (1987) claims that "One way to fight a hegemonic discourse is to teach others and ourselves alternative ways of seeing the world and discussing what it is we have come to understand as theory, research, and practice" (p. 75). Given that there were Latinas in the study, drawing on Chicana/Mexicana/Latina scholarship would have been helpful.

Fecho (2000, 2001, 2002) documents the intersections of race and class with identity and achievement as a high school English teacher–researcher in multiracial and multilingual classrooms. The English classes were housed in a Small Learning Community (SLC) within a larger, urban, predominantly African and Caribbean American high school in an impoverished Philadelphia neighborhood. Fecho draws from critical inquiry and pedagogy to examine language and identity by building upon the work of Freire (1970); responding to feminist criticisms; and embracing a continuously unfolding understanding of critical and sociocultural theory, literacy, and curriculum studies. He believes in "the importance of dialogue, both as a means for facilitating inquiry as well as a means for calling to the surface the ways class participants may feel threatened" (p. 12). His first study draws upon dialogue and students' written responses to literacy activities. He suggests that teachers do not need to seek consensus on critical issues as they create opportunities for students to make meaning of difficult issues through shared dialogue.

In a second study, Fecho (2001) addresses threats to beliefs, values, and so forth through open dialogue in a culturally diverse English classroom, when his students struggled with understanding the racial tensions between African Americans and Jews following a highly publicized tragic automobile accident. His analysis is drawn from reflective journal entries and insiders' viewpoints from the African and Caribbean American students and parents and a Jewish colleague/student teacher. Fecho uses the perspectives of others to help him gain greater insight into his data. He uses notions of border crossings and Pratt's (1991) contact zones to inform his thinking. He summarizes his underlying premise this way: "Learning and using language, therefore, involves negotiating the social context of that language, the power issues described by the language choices that are made, and complexities of making those words the language user's own" (p. 13). Likewise, Fecho (2002) conducts a close analysis of Green's (a former student of Fecho's) writing after observations, conversations, interviews, and an examination of Green's rap, essay, and op-ed piece. He interprets Green's transactions as revealing an unfolding critical consciousness with three central themes: (1) an expression of his urban life as a Black male, (2) an adoption of mainstream standards, and (3) an existential response.

Fecho draws parallels between his students' racial/ethnic, immigrant, and economic status and his own Eastern European, third-generation immigrant, working-class status, values, and upbringing. He believes that mainstream Whites do not see him as one of them. Instead, he believes he is viewed as an outsider. In his school environment, he views himself as an outsider because of the school's racial/ethnic composition and its middle-class, African American administration. He supposes that his identity markers blur the lines between a presumed privilege status of someone who looks like him—white, male, middle-class, English-dominant—and his students' life experiences, and that their similarities have helped him understand his students' lives. However, as Gilyard (2000) advises, "when we engage in discussion about fluidity, we ought to keep in mind the question of who can afford to be anchored to a focus on the indeterminate" (p. 270).

Another example of this position is seen in Sheehy's (2002) study of the co-construction of knowledge as capital and third space. She examines classroom discourse among small groups of culturally diverse middle school children, describing her work as "learning how literacy practices maintain power structures that do not allow all people to have a say in what is tasteful" (p. 285). Her description of the setting emphasizes and stereotypes socioeconomic status—including income levels, home ownership, high school completion rates, and parental status. For instance, when a student racially defines herself as "mixed . . . I'm half black, and I'm half white," Sheehy re-identifies/labels the student as African American—despite the student's self-identification as of biracial heritage (p. 288). This suggests that the researcher feels she can more accurately identify the student's race. Mischaracterizations of race extend to Sheehy's self-description as European American, middle-class, and female, oversimplifying her identity without unpacking what it means and its effect at this research site.

Throughout her presentation and analysis of the students' small-group discussions, it is clear that Sheehy's understanding of the lone African American male's interactions with his classmates is limited by her understandings of cultural and linguistic patterns and nuances. When an African American male makes a rude comment about a White girl's girth and she responds by "playing the dozens" (talking about his mama), Sheehy interprets the African American male's exchange as violent, thereby reproducing stereotypical views and values of African American males and re-centering Whiteness, normativity, and authority along Western-Eurocentric, middle-class lines of discourse. Sheehy appears to fall prey to a condition that is adequately described by Dryer (1997): "White people have power to believe they think, feel, and act like and for all people. . . . [They are] unable to see their particularity, cannot take account of other people's" (p. 9).

Rogers (2000, 2002a, 2002b, 2002c, 2003, 2004) draws from critical and feminist theoretical perspectives to understand and explain intersections of race, gender, and power within African American communities and generations of a family. Over time, she shifts her definition and description of critical literacy, CDA, and the scholarship of African Americans. Rogers gives space and depth throughout her work to descriptions of a focal African American family, and acknowledges her "cultural capital" within her position as researcher and educator. However, there is no accompanying information about Rogers's perspectives, knowledges, or predispositions or how her family life and school experiences were negotiated between home and school literacies. Rogers (2002c) claims that language is ideological, both shaped by and shaping social life, and describes the role of power in shaping and framing what constitutes school literacy and the criteria used for literacy competence. She combines broad notions of sociohistoric, economic, and cultural influences on literacy practices for students of Color, while simultaneously marginalizing specific details that are germane to the African American experience.

Rogers's (2004) study is based on a series of interviews conducted among African American adult literacy learners, where she attempts to test earlier theories, drawing on Freire's work with adult literacy programs. Her theorizing includes scholarship that envisions subjectivities beyond simple demographic categories by interrogating the "role of institutional forces in shaping social positions" (p. 276). She critiques CDA, makes conceptual expansions, and reflects on CDA's use in critical literacy research. She also includes references to the work of a large group of scholars whose lives and research reflect the spectrum of literacy research on race, class, gender, and linguistic difference. Importantly, she offers detailed information on each participant, including autobiographical sketches, and she graphically describes participants' patterns of discourse practices. Rogers notes that the participants categorized literacy learning and use at school in negative terms (an overabundance of rote learning), but their descriptions of literacy learning and use in the home and community were positive and included guided participation.

Rogers (2004) positions herself as "a Caucasian woman of Polish, Dutch, and Native American ancestry, I speak a variation of General English. I have a structured understanding of African American language" (pp. 280–281). Further, she sees herself both as an outsider who "did not share the linguistic codes of the participants" and an insider who was "a member of the school community" (p. 280). She alleges that her outsider status may have caused the participants to be more detailed in their descriptions and says that her understanding of African American interactional patterns may have helped during the interview process. She also states that her understanding of discourse patterns of directness and indirectness in African American language were helpful.

Dyson's (2003b) study also unveils an insider/outsider positioning. She examines how a group of African American 1st graders conceptualizes, uses, and adapts their ways of knowing and interacting in multiple worlds (home, school, and imaginary). The setting is a culturally and linguistically diverse urban elementary school in the eastern San Francisco Bay area. The students draw on, invent, and reinvent their worlds within a school setting, in part by re-creating levels of familial comfort and interpersonal relationships, and in part by using the home language and discourses of their young lives in school.

The entirety of the students' lives was permitted a space in the classroom—where literacy was communicated much more seamlessly and much more naturally than is typical in urban schools. Dyson (2003b) describes the way the children made sense of their worlds:

> Asked to compose "a story," to write a report about "what you learned," or simply to "write whatever you want," they drew upon familiar frames of reference and, often, old textual toys (e.g., radio songs, film dialogue, sports reports, and cartoon scenes) . . . they made new kinds of practices meaningful by infusing them with cultural knowledge and comfortable peer relations. (p. 333)

The focal group of students, an African American subset of the classroom "family structure" encouraged by their classroom teacher, formed a siblinglike bond, referring to themselves as "brothers and sisters." Dyson acknowledges that her race and age separated her from the children's experiences, yet the children label her as a "fake" mama (p. 335). The focal group informally rewrote its world through narratives and games, as well as formally when they negotiated between their fantasy world and school literacy instruction.

In this study, Dyson draws from her earlier research (Dyson, 1993), which revealed that classroom curricula should be permeable. She focuses on how the children in the study transact with the multiple forms of text and compose their own text in large part, but not exclusively, as a response to their viewing of the movie *Space Jam*. The students re-created and rewrote *Space Jam* in ongoing discussions, imaginative play, and drawings and imitated the media. She refers to the children's negotiations of recontexualizing as a way "to make a new activity meaningful." She said that "children situated that new activity within their landscape of communicative experiences. From their participation in the new activity over time, children could differentiate the possibilities and limits of particular activities" (p. 353). Dyson's extended engagement in the field led her to make several important conclusions that may well affect how language and literacy researchers engage the linguistic landscapes of children of Color: Children develop a sense of their place within their world through culture, language, and sign/symbol systems. Also, children enter into multiple relationships in which they meld all their worlds and knowledge of language, literacy, and communication to live, talk, and re-write their worlds as active language users and literacy consumers.

Williams's (2006) longitudinal study of three Black girls as they transitioned from kindergarten through 2nd grade is informed by colonial theory and CRT. She also documents changes in the girls' literacy performance and confidence as literacy producers through participant observation; parental, teacher, and student interviews; and home visits. Over time, the bright, intelligent, eager, precocious, thoughtful students who enjoyed literacy in English and Spanish became bored, ignored, and marginalized within mainstream classrooms where teachers viewed them in stereotypical ways and were not supportive of their literacy learning. Williams suggests that institutionalized discrimination and oppression thwarted some of the girls' desire to succeed.

CRITICAL PEDAGOGY

Critical pedagogy, like other forms of criticality, is evolving and being reenvisaged continually. It addresses social inequity and injustices through instruction—with the intent to develop critical consciousness by advocating for positive social change and a more democratic society. Critical pedagogues envisage classrooms and forms of instruction that acknowledge and address oppression and power domains through collective strategies and dialogue. The research in this section moves beyond theories, concepts, and methods—though they are not ignored—to praxis.

Literature, Discussion, and Popular Culture

The research in this section exhibits a commitment to social justice and educational equity through language and literacy instruction and curricular choices. As Ching (2005) admonishes, users of multicultural literature must be willing to interrogate texts in terms of history, society, politics, and power.

This body of research exhibits a commitment to social justice and educational equity through language and literacy instruction and curricular choices. Möller and Allen (2000), for instance, adopt a critical pedagogical approach to literature instruction to address social justice themes in their examination of students' responses to Mildred Taylor's (1987) *The Friendship*. The authors use critical theory, among other perspectives, to discuss and analyze the reading responses of four struggling readers, all girls of Color (three African Americans and one Latina). Their initial goal was to gain a better understanding of reader response among struggling readers. They realized that a greater understanding of critical language and discourse in reading is needed, along with an understanding of the difficulty that is involved in responding to a novel that includes issues of race, equity, and social justice. During the girls' multilayer discussions, they transacted with the text and the contexts (of community, school, and group) as they adjusted and readjusted to changes within their understanding of the history of oppression in the United States. The authors write, "realizing how intimately people are connected through language illuminates the dialogic nature of responding to literature" (p. 148). They add that it is important to create a safe space for students to express their growing critical consciousness and to address worlds beyond their own in their writing. Accordingly, Gilyard (2000) suggests the use of instruction that "encourages students to contribute through their writing fuller accounts of the world that establish contexts beyond a narrow student–teacher relationship for the dissemination of students' ideas [and] that question the implications of rhetorical choice" (p. 265). The space created by the researchers permitted the girls to dialogue with one another, even when dialogue was uncomfortable, especially as they transacted with the text and moved from fiction to their own realities. The evolving critical consciousnesses among participants and researchers is noteworthy.

Damico (2005) uses multicultural poetry to explore social justice issues in a 5th-grade classroom where students see select content in gendered terms and where writing, literature, and poetry are feminized. The careful selection of poetry elicits responses from students regarding social injustices and crosses gender lines. Glazier and Seo (2005) also acknowledge the importance of carefully selected materials, but add that it is equally important for teachers, especially monocultural White teachers, not to "reinforce notions of 'culture-lessness' among white European American student populations" (p. 686). They hold that Whiteness studies are a missing link in teacher education that leaves many White educators feeling cultureless. They encourage the creation of a transforming curriculum that seeks to help students deconstruct text and view text from multiple perspectives that include addressing inter- and intracultural understandings. The authors point to the power of discussion to support the teaching of multicultural literature from a critical perspective. For instance, Connor (2003) documents the experiences of a diverse class of high schoolers as they reflected on Tom Feelings's drawings in *The Middle Passage: White Ships/Black Cargo*. She finds that students' initial impressions changed when they were encouraged to transact with the drawings in response to critical queries. She observes that the presentation of multicultural texts must be accompanied by informed instruction if the purpose is to raise critical consciousness.

Morrell's (2004a, 2004b, 2005) body of work demonstrates how theories of criticality and cultural studies can inform pedagogy to revolutionize canonical literature by using popular culture to support the knowledges, languages, cultures, and experiences of urban youth. His research, carried out among urban adolescents of Color who live in impoverished neighborhoods and attend underfunded public schools, is informed by a careful weaving of multiple complementary assumptions that he adapts in a transformational pedagogy, or what he refers to as "the critical teaching of popular culture . . . to help students acquire and develop the literacies needed to navigate 'new century schools'" (Morrell, 2002, p. 72). He acknowledges the importance of understanding that academic language and literacy are part of the reproduction of inequities in society. However, he seeks to bridge the gap between academic and nonschool language and literacy by encouraging teachers to work toward "a radical transformation of the discipline and the practice of training English teachers" (Morrell, 2005, p. 319). He understands that language and literacy are never neutral and are always political acts that form linkages "between the literacies associated with young people's participation with popular culture and the work of secondary English classrooms" (p. 314). Areas of limitation are found in his uncritical faith in the ideas of select theorists where critique would be more appropriate and his unsteady discussion of race/ethnicity as a social construct and lived reality. His use of shifting descriptors is problematic because he asks urban youth to draw from their lived experiences as an oppressed/marginalized group of youth of Color; to reflect the intersections among race, ethnicity, class, gender, and geography within popular culture; and to interrogate domains of power, while failing to expressly address his social construction of race/ethnic as identity markers.

Morrell and Duncan-Andrade (2002, 2004) draw on urban students' knowledge of popular culture, interests, and experiences outside of school to help reform the English curriculum. Given that urban youth of Color are often depicted in the media as anti-intellectual, directionless, and unsophisticated, lacking an appreciation of culture and education, the authors offer a counterdiscourse of urban students as learners. They support the participants' learning by connecting classical poetry and contemporary forms of poetry, drawing on popular culture using hip-hop, rap, film, and mass media (Morrell & Duncan-Andrade, 2002). The authors point to the importance of considering hip-hop, especially rap music, as a literary text, as an expression of the lives of urban youth, as a form of resistance that is worthy of consideration, and as a venue for postsecondary writing. Morrell (2005) believes it is important to examine "the inherent logic and intellect of how people are literate in the world as they participate in everyday activity, [so that] we can begin to explore the potential connections between these literate behaviors and the types of literacies promoted in schools" (p. 313). Urban adolescents of Color can become critical thinkers and consumers of social thought and language, enabling them to communicate their response to local circumstances in urban, school, community, and societal contexts.

Alexander-Smith (2004) also examines the use of hip-hop as a form of popular culture in a poetry unit with her middle school students, arguing that "it communicates the reality of urban life from their perspective and it is an art form deeply rooted in their culture" (p. 58). She observes that the rhythm of hip-hop music is often used as background for spoken-word performances where "the cadence and direct language of hip-hop music . . . uplift the critical consciousness of those who listen to it" (p. 59). In addition, Cooks (2004) recognizes the use of hip-hop as a form of written and oral expression used by students in out-of-school settings, and celebrates its use and usefulness in schools. Critically conscious instructors include multicultural literature and popular culture in their curricula to address past and present oppression, inequity, and social injustices; to balance the overrepresentation of canonical literature; to deconstruct ideological assumptions of Whiteness and its superiority and legitimacy; and to disrupt universalizing ideas.

Agency and Student Voice

Cahnmann's (2005) ethnographic study examines the critical pedagogy of a Latina teacher who reenvisions an innovative space for bilingual education and the role of translation by teachers and students in school relationships. The teacher sought to debunk official images of Latino/a learners by viewing bilingual education as more than "translating the English language curriculum into Spanish but also about translating the culture of the curriculum to conform with students' identities and interests" (p. 230). She articulates a program where translation is used to share "information about identities, ideologies, and relationships between speakers, hearers, and translated material" (pp. 230–231). She also seeks to elevate the low-status image of bilingual education by establishing a transitional bilingual program between middle and high school, and a gifted bilingual education program. Cahnmann uses excerpts from one event to demonstrate how the teacher modeled her ideas using multiple levels of translation, and labels this model an "empowerment model of translation" (p. 240) that is used during the course of everyday events.

Solsken, Willett, and Wilson-Keenan's (2000) longitudinal study was conducted in grades 1–2. Their research builds upon the notion of hybridity, where critical perspectives help inform, interrogate, and transform "the knowledge, texts, and identities of the school curriculum" (p. 180). Self-identifying as White, middle-class, and female, they positioned themselves as learners who were willing to question and challenge their own ideologies and practice.

Their research project took place in an urban, culturally diverse elementary school, predominantly Puerto Rican and African American, where many students lived in poverty. Solsken et al. read widely from the available research on Puerto Rican cultural practices and sought information and insights from cultural insiders and language and literacy scholars to help them understand and interpret their data and the focal student's discourse patterns. They found a wealth of information that allowed them to understand that the student drew from multiple knowledge systems (Puerto Rican, gendered, and Western), multiple contexts and discourses (family/home, community, and school), and two languages (Spanish and English) as she constructed oral and written texts. Solsken et al. learned that the student "was able to construct different versions of her literate and fictional identities that were appropriate to the different settings in which she wrote the stories but that also incorporated aspects of identity valued in other settings" (p. 201). The authors admit that they often were unaware of how well and how often the student was able to seamlessly negotiate and apply multiple systems of knowledge, contexts, and discourses: "the richness and complexity of Blanca's stories were largely unacknowledged and unappreciated at the time" (p. 202). The researchers were proud to have been able to support the student's literacy growth and development, despite their lack of knowledge and understanding of her abilities.

Rogers, Tyson, and Marshall (2000) sought to "understand the relationship of school literacy practices to the larger discourses of literacy, families, and schooling in our neighborhoods and communities . . . [and how this] interplay both shape[s] and reflect[s] cultural practices of schooling" (p. 2). The authors recognized that their differences as people and researchers (European American female professor, African American female doctoral candidate, and European American graduate student) affected their project. They believed that their multiple subjectivities informed their understandings of the families, neighborhoods, and discourses they studied, as well as the research site, data collection, analyses, and interpretation.

The focus of their work is one African American neighborhood, two overlapping discourses, and three African American children (their families, teachers, and principals). The participating families' discourse surrounding literacy learning pointed to "economic survival" (p. 11), whereas the school personnel more broadly defined *literacy* to include aesthetic, social, and personal needs. Both groups, however, privileged school discourses over home and community discourse. Rogers, Tyson, and Marshall (2000) allege that the discourse preferences mask other, more systemic concerns. Similarly, Wynne (2002) notes that culture and language are intimately woven into the lives of users. In other words, "language is who we are.

If any of us refuse to respect the other's language, it becomes too easy, consciously or unconsciously, to then disrespect the person" (p. 212). Teacher education can support change.

Critical Pedagogy and Teacher Education

Lewis, Ketter, and Fabos (2001) explore how multicultural literature is read, understood, and incorporated in a rural, middle-class, predominantly White community in the Midwest. Their longitudinal study addressed the "political nature of selecting, interpreting, and teaching multicultural literature" (p. 315) in a community where Whiteness was envisaged as natural, normal, and desirable, but needed to be interrogated by teachers and students. The study group consisted of White female teachers and researchers who described their race and ethnicity with varying levels of explicitness. The researchers sought, with shifting commitment, to reconcile their Whiteness as they became increasingly aware of how they were "implicated in sustaining particular norms and whiteness even as we attempted to disrupt these norms" (p. 318). Throughout detailed accounts of the political and social ramifications in their community—including multicultural literature in the middle school literacy curriculum—arises a collective critical consciousness: "regulated by historical and political constructions of racial identity" (p. 325). For example, the researchers questioned how their Whiteness occludes their interpretation of characters of Color, as well as how their heterosexual identities delimited their interpretations of gender, race, and sexuality. They demonstrate how discussions of race, often spaces of resistance by teachers, move to discussions of other oppressions, particularly gender or class, or universal life experiences.

Morrell and Collatos (2002) offer an example of a critical and innovative teacher education program, the Pacific Beach Project at the University of Southern California, which aims to broaden novice teachers' understanding of and interactions with urban youth of Color. Likewise, research by R. Rogers, Kramer, Mosley, Fuller, Light, Nehart, Jones, Beaman-Jones, DePasquale, Hobson, and Thomas (2005) describes how participants in the Literacy for Social Justice Teacher Research Group transformed their thinking, instruction, and interpretation of students' lives and academic performance through their group's interactions and discussions about critical theories, pedagogy, and literature.

Critical Media Literacy and Popular Culture

Kellner and Share (2005) note the importance of employing critical and feminist theories to deconstruct and interrogate the multiple messages that are used in media. They outline key concepts of critical media literacy that include the principle of nontransparency (all media messages are constructed), codes and conventions (media messages are constructed using a creative language with its own rules), audience decoding (different people experience the same media message differently), content and message (the media have embedded values and points of view), and motivation (the media are organized to gain profit and/or power). The authors encourage the use of critical approaches with the media that "make us aware of how media construct meanings, influence and educate audiences, and impose their messages and values" (p. 371). They argue that there is a convergence among critical pedagogies and cultural studies that "involves cultivating skills in analyzing media codes and conventions, abilities to criticize stereotypes, dominant values, and ideologies, and competencies to interpret the multiple meanings and messages generated by media texts" (p. 372).

Alvermann and Xu (2003) describe popular culture and its connections to language arts instruction as they compare and contrast numerous viewpoints used to characterize popular culture as high/low culture, mass media, and folk culture. They understand *popular culture* as "everyday culture" and recognize four distinct approaches used in studying popular culture in classrooms: detrimental, critical analysis, pleasure-seeking, and self-reflexive (p. 147). Their description of teachers' and students' popular culture illustrates a narrow, White, English-dominant set of references with an obligatory reference to non-White entertainers, programs, and movies. *Popular culture* becomes redefined as mainstream culture. Although popular, it delimits what is considered "everyday culture."

Dimitriadis (2001) critiques research into popular culture and its ability to shape identity, suggesting that the more prevalent forms focus on textual analysis and resistance. In his study, two young African American males engage popular culture to support their evolving sense of social identity through biographies and relationships, both real and fictive. Dimitriadis's critical ethnography evolved from the community center where he worked, volunteered, and talked with youth. Although he acknowledges that, racially and culturally, he is an outsider to the African American community, he claims that he developed a special, unique, trusting relationship with the participants, which led them to unquestioningly share their lives, thoughts, and desires with him: "I was able, as the only white person who occupied such a position, to negotiate new kinds of relationships and trust with young people over this period . . . for more informal kinds of interactions with these young people" (p. 34). He describes the social networks of both young men, as well as their relationship with each other and their interactions with and around rap music "that reached across generations and provided them key social support in the face of ever present flux" (p. 48). Given his findings, Dimitriadis advocates for greater teacher understanding of the influence of popular culture in the lives of youth as a venue for improving education. Collins (2000) cautions that there is a growing trend among outsiders to appropriate the knowledges of insiders as their own. She writes that subjugated knowledges "develop in cultural contexts controlled by oppressed groups. Dominant groups aim to replace subjugated knowledge with their own specialized thought because they realize that gaining control over this dimension of subordinate groups' lives simplifies control" (p. 286).

SUMMARY

Critically conscious language and literacy research and pedagogy aim to deconstruct the hegemonic forces that sustain race/ethnicity, gender, language, social class, and immigrant status. The scholarship in this chapter reflects the evolving nature of criticality, with a pronounced emphasis on race/ethnicity as well as studies that center on gender, language, and sexual orientation. Critically conscious research does not require the invocation of any select group of theorists, but it does acknowledge, address, interrogate, and engage power differentials both historically and in contemporary settings. Descriptions of singular and intersecting oppression seldom reflect the historical or contemporary complexities in which they are situated. Rarely does a researcher explicate the circumstances of privilege/domination faced by participants.

The presentation of singular categories as identity markers of oppression occludes intersectionality and fails to address the matrix of domination that sustains their effect. Race is characterized simplistically by phenotype and is dichotomized as White/non-White.

Language is portrayed as English or non-English (as opposed to defaulting to Spanish). Gender is characterized as either male or female and is assumed to be White male and White female unless otherwise specified, thus re-normalizing Whiteness. Social class is characterized as related solely to income, as high, middle, or low. However, class is also related to status, which may or may not be reflective of income. Immigrant status is characterized and limited to Brown- and Black-skinned, non-English-speaking, low-income, and uneducated. It ignores White, non-English-speaking, low-income immigrants, many of whom lack formal education and work in low-paying jobs. Most critical language and literacy researchers acknowledge the race, gender, class, and language/s of participants but rarely look at sexual orientation or religion, unless these topics are the focus of study.

There are instances when race is combined with gender. However, gender is emphasized; following Whiteness, gender predominates. When gender identifiers are used in combination with students of Color, race is more predominant. Similarly, when social class is used as an identity marker, it is listed along with race, and, on occasion, gender. When race and class are combined, however, most often the reference is to urban, inner-city, poor participants of Color. Missing is any substantial body of research that features middle-class or upper-class students of Color. This supports assumptions that these participants are more like their White counterparts because they are from a similar social class. As we have demonstrated, too often, descriptions and discussions of the intersections of race and social class view status and social class as synonymous, but status is local and contextual. Status can become exacerbated when race/ethnicity, language, and sexual orientation oppression intersect. Researchers who examine race and sexual orientation often ignore race and focus instead on sexual orientation. When race, gender, and sexual orientation are identified, there is a default to the sexual orientation of Whites as a benchmark for understanding the sexual orientation of non-Whites. To ignore the ways in which issues of race/ethnicity intersect with sexual orientation is to misread the lives of the participants. When race/ethnicity/immigrant status and language are discussed, language predominates, with some mention of its intersection with class, immigrant status, and race/ethnicity.

Researchers who identify by race/ethnicity, gender, language/s, and class are unlikely to self-identify by sexual orientation or religion unless these identity markers are the foci of the study. The veneer of self-revelation based on race, class, and gender is often shortsighted—

for instance, identifying as White, middle-class, and female adds little useful information. The descriptors avoid adequate discussion of the differences between researchers and participants. Excusatory language is used to refashion the outsider positioning of White researchers as uniquely informed trusted co-learners/writers. Researchers who suggest that they have developed a very special, unique, trusted, outsider-within relationship with their participants—what we call an "internalized omniscient understanding"—thereby reposition the researcher as the holder of insider knowledge. Their positioning warrants caution, as the researchers—perhaps unwittingly—re-center Whiteness. We concede that there are trusting relationships; however, for every researcher to develop such relationships defies logic.

CHAPTER 7

Critical Language and Literacy Research in the Interpersonal Domain

I am not educated, nor am I an expert in any particular field—
but I am sincere, and my sincerity is my credentials.
—Malcolm X, "A Declaration of Independence,"
March 12, 1964

Who can/should represent the lives, experiences, and voices of the oppressed is an irresolvable debate. Collins (2003) notes, "While a piece of the oppressor may be planted deep within each of us, we each have the choice of accepting that piece or challenging it as part of the true focus of revolutionary change" (p. 340). Historically, oppressed people have expressed themselves using their languages, literacies, music, and arts, irrespective of the lack of acknowledgment and acceptance of dominant groups. Critically conscious research seeks to liberate the voices of the oppressed, "when people reclaim their language and, with it, the power of envisagement, the imagination of a different world . . . [is] brought into being" (Berhoff, 1987, p. xv). It is through the interpersonal realm that individual and collective narratives speak to the capacity of individuals to use their language/s and literacies to name their realities and to work toward social transformation. There are a limited number of narratives and counternarratives published in the mainstream language and literacy professional journals, making it difficult to pinpoint when this institutional marginalization began, but it plagues the field and delimits research that might otherwise revolutionize inquiry. Studies by scholars of Color offer exemplary narrative and counternarratives from an insider perspective, along with the work of well-informed White allies.

Collins (2000) describes the interpersonal domain as being reflective of "discriminatory practices of everyday lived experience that because they are so routine typically go unnoticed or remain unidentified" (p. 299). Her characterization informs our review and critique of scholarship in this chapter, where individuals express how intersections of oppression have shaped their lives or the lives of their participants and describe how structures (historic, societal, cultural, and instructional) inhibit and constrain voice. This body of research describes the ways that researchers have tackled the interpersonal domain on multiple levels. We begin with a brief overview of narrative construction in light of critically conscious research, followed by our review and critique.

Narrative Construction

Narratives, whether written, spoken, or performed, are part of our meaning-making as individuals and collective groups. Gramsci (1971) predicted, "the starting point of critical elaboration is the consciousness of what one really is" (p. 323). Contemporary scholars who express the importance of narrative include Apple (1999), who declares that narratives are "spaces for the embodied voice of the silenc*ed* (the stress of the last two letters is important . . . it signifies an active process of control, regulation, and policing) to be articulated" (p. x, italics in original). Chase (2005) poses the following questions about narratives:

> What kinds of narratives disrupt oppressive social processes? How and when do researchers' analyses and representations of others' stories encourage social justice and democratic processes? And for whom are these processes disrupted and encouraged? Which audiences need to hear which researchers' and narrators' stories? (p. 667)

Criticalists' use of narrative is respectful of the history of oppression and does not rely on unproven, albeit commonly accepted, stereotypes of the "Other" to characterize the experiences of participants who opt to allow their voices to speak (Orellana, 2001). Insider points of view also inform the way narratives are communicated. Willis (2005) articulates that language and literacy research by scholars of Color must invoke a reclamation and "de-Othering" of people of Color as an acknowledgment of selfhood, completeness, and humanity.

Brayboy (2000), a member of the Lumbee-Cheraw tribe, acknowledges: "I have come to realize that how we define our subjects and ourselves is important in the data we collect, analyze, and publish" (p. 424). Introspectively, he details the struggles that Indigenous researchers face as academics and members of the communities in which they conduct their research. His initial concerns about identity and authenticity relied on physical and linguistic characteristics, blood percentages, tribal affiliation, and political sensibilities but have evolved to "recognize the forces that have led us to differentiate among ourselves in such specific and destructive ways" and "examine how issues around colonialism influence the ways in which we essentialize each other" (p. 425). He is not alone; Grande (2000b) recalls her struggle with identity and authenticity as an Indian and has come to realize that "the notion of the 'authentic' Indian is a myth constructed and perpetuated by Whitestream America" (p. 348).

Baquedano-Lopez (2004) also recalls her inner struggle and tension when her position as a researcher abutted her personal space as a native Spanish-language speaker, first-generation immigrant, and Catholic: "I publicly identified as a member of the community on the occasions I joined the Spanish-speaking Latino leaders in confronting exclusionary statements from non-Latino members in the face of increasing marginalizing educational practices" (p. 216). Her disclosure supports Madison's (2005) contention that this form of research "takes us beneath surface appearances, disrupts the status quo, and unsettles both neutrality and taken-for-granted assumptions by bringing to light underlying and obscure operations of power and control" (p. 5). In this case, the personal is political, and the political is personal.

Delgado Bernal (2001) shares the importance of memory and narrative in Chicana feminist pedagogy, noting that the use of "community and family knowledge is taught to youth through such ways as legends, *corridos*, storytelling, and behavior" (p. 624). Haig-Brown (2003) argues for the use of *testimonio* in written and oral forms, as well as a method that includes observation, interviewing, and listening to craft narrative, because they "may allow people to tell their stories with less intervention, interruption, and interpretation than do typical interviews, even when they are thought to be open-ended, feminist, critical, and/or anti-racist" (p. 416). She indicates that one of the enduring features of *testimonio* "is the fact that the life story presented is not simply a personal matter; rather it is the story of an individual who is also part of a community" (p. 420). These communities typically do not have access to academia or broad public distribution of their stories. Haig-Brown asks whose voice is heard in constructing *testimonio*; how does one retain and respect the "voice," the "story," and the experiences of the interviewee when writing for academic purposes? Although she does not resolve this dilemma, she maintains that *testimonio* offers greater space for change within the academy: "Being open to new knowledge forms and striving to find new ways of resisting the imposition of culturally and linguistically inhibiting structures upon what we hear and/or read can affect constructions of knowledge within the academe" (p. 418). The interpersonal domain offers a space where individual and collective knowing can be nurtured, grown, and affirmed.

Narratives written from a CRT perspective "emphasize aesthetic and emotional dimensions in their stories to stimulate the imagination and to inspire empathy to allow others to imagine the mind of the oppressed and to see, and perhaps vicariously experience, the world through their eyes" (Duncan, 2005, p. 102). The individual and group voices of oppressed people are especially qualified to tell their own stories, without essentializing experiences to all group members. For example, Behar's (2001) innovative use of autobiography and ethnography highlights intersections of oppression, as seen in her novel *Nightgowns from Cuba*. She crosses many borders, both literal and figurative, in her creative use of narrative, which challenges notions of race/ethnicity, class, gender, and power in pre-Castro Cuba.

Narratives of
Researchers and Teacher Educators

The biographical nature of this domain is most clearly expressed in personal narratives as people trace their inner language and literacy journeys. Through providing seemingly familiar details to enrich their narratives, scholars offer a greater understanding of their sociohistoric contexts. Honeyghan (2000) uses personal memories of life in a Jamaican village to locate multiple sources of literacy that are informed by culture, language, and funds of knowledge. She specifically draws upon her remembrances of the sounds of life in a rural village: oral storytelling; songs sung by villagers; music (local musicians, U.S. soul music, and reggae); the rhythms of home, school, and church; the recitation of poems; and literature. She recalls that "stories told to me as a child taught morals, traditions, and traditional values . . . an integral part of African culture—linked to the history of slavery and the survival of the human psyche" (p. 411). She also observes, "When I write, I find myself recording the Creole . . . my strongest voice is in the village lingo. . . . [M]y deepest thought processes are bound up in the structure of the Creole, in the voices that surrounded me, that reached within me" (p. 412). Honeyghan articulates that her early en-trée into literacy began with the rhythms of her early life (before formal schooling) and continue to be a part of her innermost thoughts, understandings, and perspectives.

Dowdy (2002) situates her narrative in the sociohistoric events and the migratory history and genetic influences of Trinidadians whose genetic roots and linguistic routes stem from the coast of West Africa and include language patterns from Europe, India, and Asia —all part of a complex linguistic heritage. She remembers that the pressure to adopt formal English meant that:

> Your job, as a survivor of the twenty-odd generations of slaves and indentured workers and overseers, is to be best at the language that was used to enslave you and your forebears. It is a painful strategy for survival, but maybe it is just another facet of the kind of transcendence to which the descendants of kidnapped Africans had to aspire in order to survive the very memory of slavery. (p. 7)

She draws from life experiences, arguing that the push to acquire formal/academic English became a psychological burden: "I now saw that the linguistic tension that I lived every day was the result of a war for the minds of the colonized. I came to understand that the colonizer only valued the native language of the colonized in the realm of entertainment" (p. 11). Further, she presents the tension experienced by forced/coerced language dominance: "Everyone who writes the language, knows that they have to translate their thoughts as fast as they can speak, if they are going to come across as more than morons attempting to speak" (p. 7). The importance of her linguistic history helped shape her identity and perspectives on language and literacy instruction.

The experiences of Honeyghan and Dowdy support a warning from McCarty et al. (2005): "Indigenous languages (like other minority languages) are increasingly threatened by the forces of globalization—cultural, economic, and political forces that work to standardize and homogenize, even as they stratify and marginalize" (p. 2). These narratives demonstrate reflexively that the instantiation of familial, social, and community beliefs and values, as well as everyday conversations, comments, encounters, and other sources of information (e.g., media images), greatly impact language and literacy learning.

Researcher and Teacher Educator Personal Narratives

Klevan (2002), a graduate student, does not self-identify or share any particular theoretical/conceptual framework that guides his writing, as he recalls how his preconceived notions about "inner-city" high schools, student achievement, and bilingual education evolved during his research in an El Paso, Texas, high school. His narrative is informed by field notes and journals that he kept during his research project, revealing how he was forced to deal with his own racial, ethnic, class, and linguistic demons and stereotypes. Klevan admits to having little prior interaction with students who attended inner-city schools, and passive acceptance of images promoted by the media depicting inner-city schools, teachers, and students as violent, unmotivated, unfocused, and unintelligent.

He describes a turning point in his thinking when his preconceived notions about a student who spoke English fluently caused him to assume that the student was an advanced learner, middle-class, and a "good" student. The student had been homeless, was fluent in both Spanish and English, and was considered a troublemaker. Klevan realized that he had judged the student based on his English proficiency, assuming that "English-speaking students are the high achievers in bilingual education . . . [and] those who speak Spanish are the ones who struggle in school" (p. 51). His relationships with teachers and students helped him reconcile his own stereotypes and prejudices, which were informed by media images and test results. He acknowledges that he had to address his "own complicity in the problem . . . concentrating on the damage imposed by the structure while remaining blind to the power of human agency to challenge the structure" (p. 49). His narrative highlights the countless stereotypes that we all carry with us, consciously and unconsciously, which affect our interactions, actions, intentions, and misunderstandings of those who are different from ourselves.

Pilcher (2001) recalls her attempts as a White teacher educator to provide a space for discussion of Black women's voices in an entry-level qualitative research course taught simultaneously online and face-to-face. She sought to help her 32 students (5 African American women, 1 African American male, and 26 White males and females) better understand notions of domination. Pilcher's course consisted of writings by African American women authors and scholars and opportunities to write and "talk" (online). The students' responses to readings and postings included anger, resistance, caring, personalization, and silence. Pilcher weaves their voices among commentary and analysis to explain her decision making, comfort level, doubts, fears, guilt, and triumphs. Pilcher was surprised that her attempt to provide a space for Black women's voices was met with silence by Black women. Later, she met with the Black women students and a Black female faculty member on a weekly basis to engage and challenge the unresolved issues in the course. There, the Black women openly shared how they met, struggled, and survived challenges in their personal lives and the oppressions that were a part of their lives as African American women in the South and as daughters and friends. Pilcher experienced clarity regarding the standpoints of the Black women, saying that "living through our own and one another's critical consciousness in our everyday lives affords us opportunities for revolutionizing change" (p. 299). Her social transformation continues to evolve.

Asher (2005), who was raised in India, self-identifies as international but recognizes that in the United States, this translates into being labeled a minority. She prefers a hybrid sense of self as "academic Self-woman of color Other" (p. 1086). Her research examines critical multiculturalism and pedagogy through student autobiographies. Asher believes that it is important in our global society for students to be exposed to and learn how to deconstruct "the colonizer and external oppressive structures, but also one's own internalization of and participation in the same" (p. 1080). Her analysis of her Southern White students' autobiographies reveals everyday experiences in which the students have shared subtle and not-so-subtle comments about African Americans. These experiences reveal how race (integration, segregation, and fear) and religious denominations (Catholics, Protestants, and Christians) have impacted their lives in both conscious and unconscious ways.

Aveling (2001), another teacher educator, speaks as "a white woman living in Australia coming from a migrant background" (p. 35). She presents autobiographical snippets in what she calls "critical storytelling" to explain how her identity has evolved (p. 37). She believes that discussions of Whiteness are necessary components of critical pedagogy and teacher education where Whiteness is epitomized in history, symbolized in language, and glorified in culture. Reflecting on her life as an immigrant in Australia through finely grained memories, she addresses her evolving sense of self, race, and Whiteness, while simultaneously avoiding comparisons of her oppression ("me-too-isms" that re-center Whiteness) with that of Australia's Indigenous population. With great care, she recalls hearing and feeling that "being 'black' meant you were different: where difference was beginning to be firmly defined as 'not like me.' . . . I never thought of myself as 'white;' being 'white' was simply not an issue" (p. 38). Throughout her schooling, Aboriginal people were described and discussed historically, not as a living people. Aveling shares her autobiographical writing with her students as a starting point for them to examine their past and the present, and to prepare for the future.

Marker (2000) uses narratives to explicate a history of strained Indian-White relations in a Pacific Northwest community that adversely affects the education of the Lummi children who attend local public schools and a nearby predominantly White university: "The struggles are embedded in the politics of Indian–White relations in the region surrounding the university. The university is mired in the ways power and language have defined and confined the local tribal people" (p. 403). Early interviews among the Lummi helped Marker understand how important the collective memory of Indigenous people is in helping to guide their interactions. He learns of strong anti-Indian sentiments in the area, which are based in part on fishing rights, the perception of unearned entitlements granted to the Lummi by the federal government, and a pipeline of racist teacher educators from the local university who complete their student teaching in local schools under equally racist and insensitive faculty and who later may teach in local schools. He writes that the university "played a large role in perpetuating stereotypes and negative attitudes about Indians" (p. 409). From interviews with Whites, mostly university faculty and local classroom teachers, he finds historical amnesia surrounding the tense Indian–White relations and silence from faculty members, who openly use racist descriptions of the Lummi and their alleged inferior genetic/inherited intellectual ability. Marker concludes that Whites' lack of historical memory helps explain "the ways that knowledge/power is maintained by neutralizing the past and confiscating the constructed present" (p. 411).

Reed (2003), a White female scholar, seeks to understand how people define their identity in the racially/ethnically diverse chain of the Hawaiian Islands. Her longitudinal study among pre- and in-service teachers reveals variations within the group. She believes that a people's locale plays a role in how that people identifies their heritage, although her interviews were conducted among predominantly Asian female college students. Lefcourt (2005, 2006), a member of the royal Hawaiian bloodline, argues that Native Hawaiians see the inhabitants of Hawai'i differently. Indigenous peoples of Hawai'i do not express confusion over their identities in the same way that Reed's interviewees do. She claims that Indigenous understanding of identity centers on their belief that they are of the `*aina* (land): They come from the land, so there is no question about their identity. She also believes that Indigenous Hawaiians know who they are and don't need to ask the question "Who am I?" (personal communication, 11/08/06).

Aguirre (2005) also uses narrative inquiry to describe the changing role of Chicano faculty in academe. He acknowledges that he "carried in my mind and heart my migrant farm worker life" (p. 148). He observes Chicano faculty who face the same oppression that Chicanos/as face in the larger society. The walls of the ivory tower of academe do not shield them from discrimination. Displays of power and domination range from the consistent mispronunciation of Chicano surnames to attempts to pigeonhole research interests. In addition, he uses personal narratives as part of his teaching to help students uncover, demystify, and challenge master narratives and notions of equity, social justice, and democracy.

Counternarratives of Schoolchildren of Color

Yosso (2005b) articulates that a counternarrative "recounts experiences of racism and resistance from the perspectives of those on society's margins" (p. 2). She has identified three specific forms of counternarratives: autobiography, biography, and composite. Counternarratives help students work against racelessness, which Fordham (1988) defines as "culturally sanctioned interactional and behavioral styles" (p. 54). According to Fordham, students "adopt those styles [that are] rewarded in the school context if they wish to achieve academic success" (p. 55). Stacey Lee (2004) observes that in the 21st century, in racially, ethnically, and linguistically diverse classrooms, "whiteness remains the ubiquitous norm against which students of Color are judged" (p. 121). Further, she writes that men of Color, from children to young adults, are often "criminalized in the mainstream imagination" while Asian American males are often portrayed as the antithesis of African American and Latino males (p. 121). These socially constructed views of males of Color affect the ways in which they are perceived and educated.

Quiroz (2001) and L. Fernández (2002) use counternarratives to debunk the stereotypical image of Latina/o students that is found in much of the research they draw from student autobiographies to demonstrate the perceptions and realities of Latino/a students' educational journeys. Quiroz's ethnographic study uses narratives to better understand the lives of 27 Latina/o (Mexican and Puerto Rican) students in an economically depressed and socially isolated portion of a large urban school. The district requires students to write an autobiography in 8th grade and repeat the process in 11th grade. These autobiographies focus on "students' views of family, school, ethnicity, and future plans" (p. 327). Although the counselors and teachers at the high school know that the autobiographies are part of the students' records, they seldom read them. The autobiographies reveal "scenarios of schooling and critiques of the educational experience" as explained by the students who are living through them (p. 327). Quiroz's stance is critical as she seeks to advocate for the lives of children. The autobiographical narratives represent student voices and are a "window into the seemingly intractable dropout rates of Latino children, the reasons behind their academic decisions, and the interventions needed to change these persistently unfavorable directions" (pp. 328–329). School counselors and teachers largely ignore the students' autobiographies, except in instances of misbehavior, which suggests school-sponsored silencing, where administrators, teachers, and staff control who speaks, under what conditions, and in what discourse (Fine, 1991). Quiroz observes that there are differences based on ethnicity, English fluency, and immigration status, as well as similarities in experience that define "the quandaries and paradoxes of prejudice, paternalism, or personal dissonance, and their effects on identity" (p. 335). She also notes how the autobiographies trace identity formation around experiences and labels, associated with participation in bilingual classes. The negative impact of high teacher mobility causes students to internalize failure and causes shifts in future plans from fantasizing about grandiose ideas to practical ones.

In another instance, L. Fernández's (2002) analysis of one student's school autobiography is informed by CRT and LatCrit theories and acknowledges that the narratives she reads have been written as schoolwork. Her informant, Pablo, supplies information about his schooling by describing the lack of academic rigor, teacher attitudes toward and low expectations for Spanish-speaking students, experiences in bilingual education, and racialized discourses, instruction, materials, and counseling. Because these experiences were largely negative, he also recalls how students learned to resist dominant ideologies by cutting class and dropping out. Fernandez surmises, "although his classmates may not have consciously realized the racist practices that victimized them, they understood to some extent that the school was not serving them adequately or equitably" (p. 58).

Otoya-Knapp (2004) self-identifies as "a Peruvian heterosexual woman who immigrated to the United States at 9 years of age" (p. 155). She examines student autobiographies in a racially diverse high school in Los Angeles where students "engage in critical inquiry about their experiences and how they are affected by race, class, gender, and power issues" (p. 150). She held monthly sessions that allowed students to "problematize the 'normal,' and participate in the democratic processes of reinventing and rethinking the possibilities of society" (p. 150). Transcripts of these sessions reveal a growing critical consciousness among the predominantly Latina/o students, who initially were hesitant to publicly speak about issues of race. Eventually, they voiced their opinions both orally and in writing. The participants relayed family conversations in which values and beliefs were discussed, ranging from colorblindness to expressions of Color awareness or sensitivity. As students become more aware of the structural inequalities that affected their lives and the informal discriminatory processes against ableness, they sought to end unfair treatment. Otoya-Knapp submits that critical inquiry is a necessary addition to high school curricula, as it allows students a place and a space to voice their growing consciousness of power, race, class, and gender inequalities. Similarly, hooks (1989) declares:

> Moving from silence into speech is for the oppressed, the colonized, the exploited, and those who stand and struggle side by side a gesture of defiance that heals, that makes new life, and new growth possible. It is that act of speech, of "talking back," that is no mere gesture of empty words, that is the expression of our movement from object to subject—the liberated voice. (p. 9)

Monzó and Rueda (2003) also draw on the funds-of-knowledge concept (Moll, Armanti, Neff, & Gonzalez, 1992), extending it to include "multifaceted relationships [and] grounded connections of *confianza* (trust)" (p. 74, italics in original). They use critical, ethnographic, and narrative methods to examine a Latina paraeducator's "funds of knowledge," specifically the ways in which she uses knowledges and languages to support students' learning and help them understand the social structures of the school that threaten to hamper their progress. The narratives of the paraeducator's life reveal that she was "a low-income Mexican immigrant child" who went to school in the United States (p. 75). Like many immigrants, her experiences include cultural alienation, separation from family, economic hardships, and discrimination and prejudice. Her life and school experiences are helpful in her support of student learning, as she draws upon shared language, culture, and experiences. For this paraeducator, "culture and language are closely intertwined with identity, social relationships, status, and other related factors and can mediate school experiences in significant ways. . . . [L]anguage and culture frequently become the media of marginalization" (p. 83). The authors trumpet the use of their extended notion of funds of knowledge to include the notion of trust in support of transformative change in language and literacy education.

Storytelling by Parents and Family Members

Delgado-Gaitan (2005) studied two groups of Latina mothers—those seeking to support their adolescent daughters in public schools and members of a support group for terminally ill children. Each group formed its own sense of community and served as a safe space for members to share personal narratives. She emphasizes the importance of this space in their lives: "to be able to name one's experience is part of what it means to 'read' the world . . . and to understand the critical nature of the limits and possibilities that make up the larger society" (p. 266). Delgado-Gaitan draws from the work of Freire, particularly the concept of *metadolgia dialectia,* where "the participants' knowledge about their daily lives forms the basis for theorizing social capital and social action addressing the conditions in which we live" (p. 267). She explains that the participants' group experiences, especially the sharing of personal narratives and ongoing life experiences, helped empower mothers and expanded their vision for their own lives and the lives of family members. She claims that stories "are part of a longer narrative of survival, of wars in distant homelands, of isolation, of illness, of poverty, and of courage . . . to preserve the thread that defines us" (p. 271). Her activist engagement with Latino immigrant families recognizes the ways in which family literacy, social inequalities, and power relations impact Latinos in public schools.

Li (2003) exposes features of the counternarratives of Chinese Canadian family members, examining how "different socioeconomic, linguistic, cultural, and political factors of cross-cultural living have contributed to their difficulties with schooling" (p. 183). He uses counternaratives to debunk narratives that align with the dominant culture, their views of immigrant acculturation processes, and the Asian "model minority" myth. His perspective is informed by his experiences in China and Canada, and he states that he is aware of how literacy is viewed and understood in each country.

He observes the parents' low educational backgrounds, their dependency on their children to help navigate and negotiate the English language, and their isolation from other Chinese Canadians. Their stories detail experiences of cultural discontinuity between their Chinese and Canadian understandings of public education, literacy, and special education/disabilities programs, as well as overt and covert forms of racism in society and within schools. He reveals that the parents' understanding of literate behaviors are "rooted in the traditional Chinese philosophy that emphasizes the ability to read classic literature. This belief was different from the Canadian school practice of using children's picture books to help foster their children's interest in reading" (p. 195). Of grave importance is the way that English-dominant societies offer access to English language learning, which Li believes should not be limited to immigrant children, but should include all children who need support. He declares, without apology, that he views his work as advocacy for immigrant families as they interact and live within social and political power structures.

Similarly, Villenas (2001) presents Latina mothers as women who understand their identity and the purposes of schooling in culturally significant ways, contrary to mainstream perceptions of their understandings in a small North Carolina town. Mainstream perceptions indicate that the Latino community is in need of the services provided by White mainstream society and that Latina mothers are in need of help to better feed, educate, and care for their families. A cultural deficit perception permeates the media and the psyche of mainstream society. Latina mothers resent and resist these perceptions and see themselves as intelligent, knowing mothers who are able to care for their children's physical and emotional needs as they seek a moral and intellectual education for their children.

The mothers' counternarratives "claimed dignity in their roles as mothers/educators who imparted what they believed to be a 'better' education of morals and values" than what is found in local schools and public services (p. 4). Villenas adds that "the mothers' complex narratives of education involved the claiming of *el hogar* (the home space) as 'educated' women responsible for the cultural preservation of a newly forming Latino community in the South" (p. 4, italics in original). The intersection of race, class, immigrant status, gender, and language is apparent in their narratives, in which they share "stories of discrimination and daily indignities" (p. 21). From a LatCrit perspective, Villenas recognizes that the migration of Latinos/as (Mexican immigrants) to the Southeastern United States is a recent phenomenon that has engendered racist attitudes "linked to the histories of colonialism and imperialism in the Americas, current immigration control policies, the changing structure of local and global markets, and the stratification of labor" (p. 5). The changing population is accompanied by a restatement of Whiteness as the standard, a racing of all non-Whites as inferior, and unlawful discrimination practices in housing, jobs, and social life.

Auberach (2002) shares the life stories of four Latino parents who participated in a program called Futures and Families, which was attended by school administrators and teachers. The parents' opportunity to share their stories helped to validate "not only their credibility . . . but also their identity as individuals within a faceless high school bureaucracy" (p. 1376). Her research reveals three types of narratives used by the parents: "life stories of parents' struggle with schooling as students; stories of bureaucratic rebuff in parents' encounters with school staff as parents; and counterstories that challenge official narratives of schooling" (p. 1370). Their counternarratives exposed fallacies about Latino/a college aspirations, power struggles over decision making in the lives of Latino/a students, institutional racism, and structural inequities in school policies and procedures.

Knight, Norton, Bentley, and Dixon (2004) share similar findings when the experiences of families of Color become part of the schooling process. The intersectionality of race, class, gender, and language in the lives of family members becomes part of the college-going process as the notion of family is redefined beyond the nuclear: "counterstories highlight youth's daily realities, including family involvement with siblings, cousins, aunts, uncles, guardians, grandparents, and other family members in college-going processes" (p. 100). Their counterstories, and the retelling of life stories by the participants, allow Knight and colleagues to reframe and revise parental/

family involvement in the college-going process. The authors note that "counterstories worked against the traditional representations of these families as deficient, disinterested, with confused priorities, and responsible for their youth's failure to enter college" (p. 100). This ethnographic study, informed by critical and feminist perspectives, involved a multiracial research team and adolescent co-researchers within a multiracial/multilingual high school class of 9th graders.

Majors (2004) uses CRT, CDA, and NLS to analyze oral narratives of African American talk among women in a Midwestern hair salon and shares the voices and life experiences of the women in the hair salon to uncover "how they construct their own countertexts in response to (social) readings" (p. 182). She reveals how her life experiences, understandings, and knowledges informed and shaped her understanding of language use and her "reading" of the participants. Majors posits that oral narrative skills are part of a person's repertoire of literacy skills and that identities and understandings, especially African American Vernacular English (AAVE), are seldom recognized or valued by mainstream researchers. She believes that these community practices and the use of language improve reading "as they extend the definition of what a text is, who a reader is, and how one talks back to disempowering readings" (pp. 170–171). Her ideas are supported by the scholarship of other female scholars of Color (Lawrence-Lightfoot, 1994; Silko, 1996) who punctuate their writing with the importance of storytelling for psychological survival and recognition.

Language and Literacy as Performance

Fisher (2003) links literacy and performance in her study of spoken-word poetry and expression within African Diaspora participatory literacy communities (ADPLC). Her study is informed by concepts found in African epistemology (NOMMO), CT, and CRT. She examines race, the African Diaspora, oppression, identity, agency, resistance, and power in the language and literacy lives of the participants. The language and literacy events in this study were conducted among people of African descent in two spoken-word venues (Oakland and Sacramento, CA) where Fisher was a participant and observer of open-mic events. She presents a wide range of voices that represent the African Diaspora and enhance the global and introspective nature of the venues. The spoken-word venues serve as sites for expression in multiple languages and literacies "because they combine oral, aural, and written traditions of people of African descent and have the potential for advancing theories that attempt to relate use of these modes of language as literacy practices" (p. 363). She links these ideas to West African communities, where audiences participate in music, sound, and verbal and nonverbal means of communication. Of particular import are the views shared by the males who participated in the study, sharing their journeys and transitions from writing rhymes to writing and performing poetry. Fisher argues that the performances represent stories within stories, as the audience has a role in the performance and the performers may respond to and perform in conjunction with the interactions of the audience. These literacy forms, oral literature and oral art, are used to share information, pass on history and culture, and critique the imposition of imperialism and colonization.

Drawing from this same body of data, Fisher (2004) examines and highlights the history and legacy of literacy among people of African Diaspora, much as King (1992) does. She places a special emphasis on orality as a form of literacy used in formal and informal settings and in community spaces by participants, who, "while refuting monolithic views of Blackness . . . reclaim orality as part of their tradition and believe it to be an extension of the written word" (pp. 292—293). Fisher articulates that people of African descent believe there is power in spoken and written words. She is not alone in her understanding of the power of the spoken word, expressionism, or the reach of the orality within the African Diaspora.

The importance of "finding one's voice" cannot be overstated. hooks (1989) observes: "[F]inding a voice is an essential part of liberation struggle—for the oppressed, a move in the direction of freedom" (pp. 17–18). By way of example, Lefcourt's (2005) critical performance ethnography bridges crevices among theory, research, and instruction. She interviewed Native Hawaiian priests, elders, and community leaders to gain their perspective on what should constitute Native Hawaiian education. In addition, she interviewed former and current teachers, administrators, and students to gain their perspectives. In the end, she presents rich, detailed narratives that describe the quality of Native Hawaiian education that is expected, accepted, and resisted.

Summary

Narrative, as method and form, can be used to nurture and foster critical consciousness, support meaning making, share cultural knowledge, create new knowledge, reclaim voices and identities, and detail lived experiences. Many well-intended researchers have represented the experiences, languages, lives, and voices of oppressed people in the academy; others have co-opted the narratives of the oppressed in a type of "academic identity theft" and have told the stories they want to believe. Still others, members of oppressed groups, speak now for themselves and members of their groups, as academics and activists.

Counternarratives offer a venue for previously faceless, name-less, and voiceless oppressed people to state and reclaim our selves, our cultures, our languages, and our literacies from the images, stereotypes, and mischaracterizations of the oppressor. This body of research explicates how multiple consciousnesses and literacies are used to validate the lives of oppressed people. Counternarratives also help reveal intersectionality, adding clarity to the ways in which multidimensional identities are formed and showing how they are necessary for survival both within and outside of academe, communities, and institutions.

Afterword

Revolution begins with the self, in the self.
—Bambara, 1970, p. 109

We began this book by acknowledging the roots and routes, historical antecedents, controversies, debates, and fissures within critical
theorizing. We have traced and documented the thinking of critical social theorists to illustrate the ideological shifts and recurring
themes in the field because we believe that critical consciousness
is ever-evolving. As Lawrence et al. (1993) articulated, "even as we
understand and name the world we see, it changes and must be understood and named again" (p. 11). Critically conscious research
continues to challenge power, inequality, social injustice, and the
reproduction of the ideas and values of dominant groups. This new
era, however, focuses on how systems of domination work to sustain
oppressive conditions and moves race/ethnicity and gender from the
shadows of critical theorizing to its center.

Re-envisioning Critically Conscious Research

We applaud the tremendous work and activism that critical language
and literacy researchers have undertaken to improve theory and praxis.
To re-envisage critical language and literacy, we begin by summarizing
what we have learned and follow with suggestions for change.

Our review and critique suggests that:

- Theoretically, there is a marginalization of primary sources
  and an over-reliance on secondary and tertiary sources,

which serves to gloss over histories and debates within the field. Moreover, too often, research that is focused on hegemony and on how institutions sustain or resist equity and social justice in language and literacy instruction is not accompanied by suggestions for change.

- Few studies include discussions of the interlocking systems of power domains and how they support or sustain social injustice and inequity.
- Studies that focus on race/ethnicity and gender oppressions predominate.
- Numerous researchers focus on a particular form of oppression and are unaware of or unwilling to address the intersectionality of oppression. It is important to address and balance singularity and intersectionality. Focusing on a singular oppression delimits an understanding of the interlocking systems of domination.
- Identity markers are used as categories of analysis, resulting in mischaracterized and essentialized units of analysis. Seldom are these identity markers deconstructed or explained within their sociohistoric contexts. Moreover, identity markers are too often described as binaries and accompanied by deficit discourse that paints participants and their communities in stereotypical ways.
- When the scholarship of non-dominant groups is acknowledged, usually an apparently obligatory reference to one or two prominent scholars, it is not engaged or interrogated. It is nearly incomprehensible for advocates of the oppressed to continually repress the voices of scholars from these groups, thereby replicating ideological domination and cultural alienation by marginalizing, ignoring, and silencing scholarship that would better inform research and praxis.
- Many studies appear to be fixated on relaying the empathic responses of teachers and researchers. This risks dehumanizing the participants and re-centers the research on the coming of critical consciousness of the researcher. Other researchers paint a rosy or romanticized picture of suffering, oppression, and teaching under stressful conditions.
- Some researchers claim to have uncovered "new" knowledges and cultural understandings of people whose lives are outside of their cultural/ethnic/linguistic frames of reference. Statements of "insider" knowledge should be used sparingly.

- Claiming what "we" in the field know or do not know about the language and literacy of underserved students is troubling. It is not clear whom "we" are, but discussions of "we" default to White, middle-class, heterosexual, and English-dominant.
- Alleged k/new knowledges are being appropriated as part of the intellectual property of White researchers, thus re-enslaving and re-colonizing the languages, literacies, and lives of the participants.
- Often, well-intentioned researchers draw from a small group of like-minded researchers within the field and perpetuate a comfortableness that does not require them to engage a broader, more diverse, and more appropriate criticality. Research by Whites among students of Color, for example, primarily draws from the work of other White researchers, thereby undermining change and advocacy and perpetuating Whiteness as "internalized omniscience."

We have used Collins's (1990, 2000) matrix of domination as an analytical tool to critique critical language and literacy research because it provides a paradigmatic shift for future critical language and literacy researchers. Collins's model also offers a more complex understanding of how systems of oppression operate and are sustained. Finally, it points out how everyone is involved in the process by demonstrating that we are all affected by systems of oppression as well as privilege. In the section that follows, we suggest first steps toward re-envisioning critical language and literacy research.

First Steps

- Critical language and literacy research should include clear statements about the roots and routes embraced by researchers. Scholars can expose their strengths and limitations as they move beyond rhetoric to wrestle with deeply rooted issues that have haunted our nation's psyche and influenced educational access, opportunities, and outcomes.
- Theoretical references should acknowledge or engage epistemologies within the participants' cultural and familial backgrounds. Research that fails to do so contributes to a type of academic imperialism for personal or professional

gain. Research could be strengthened by engaging and interrogating the theories, concepts, methods, and analytical frameworks of scholars of Color and feminist, Indigenous, and gender scholars. This is especially true when researchers engage participants from groups while focusing on identity, power, voice, and social justice.

- Researchers should clarify, define, and describe their use of the term *identity*. This term is used as a tambour where the identity of participants is stretched to conform to dominant ideas and values. The focus on identity often occludes discussions of domination by White, native English speakers from middle-class, heterosexual circumstances, which re-privileges Western-Eurocentric conceptions of critical consciousnesses. Adopting this stance also marginalizes or ignores the critical consciousnesses of scholars of Color— paradoxically, often while working to enhance the identity of participants of Color.

- The growth of multiple literacies and modalities is indeterminable but should not be unchallenged. We appreciate research that acknowledges and values, as well as critically analyzes, the production and consumption of media. We urge researchers to be open to multiple literacies and modalities and to guard against institutionalizing narrow definitions and descriptions of what constitutes popular culture.

- Caution should be used by all researchers who punctuate their text with anecdotes to convince readers that they have a unique relationship with students/participants that gives them a special insight into participants' worlds, while simultaneously minimizing, downplaying, or ignoring the importance and influence of the researcher's presence in the process.

- Researchers should become more self-reflective and should work *in cooperation with*, and not *for*, their study participants.

Critically conscious language and literacy research is defined by a commitment to equity, social justice, and the valuing of multiple languages and literacies. We believe that critical language and literacy research needs to adopt and adapt more appropriate and complex theoretical and analytical models in order to move forward. By acknowledging intersecting systems of domination, scholars in the field will be better positioned to transform and revolutionize critically conscious language and literacy research.

References

Abu-El-Haj, T. R. (2002). Contesting the politics of culture, rewriting the boundaries of inclusion: Working for social justice with Muslim and Arab communities. *Anthropology and Education Quarterly, 33*(3), 308–316.

Aguirre, A. (2005). The personal narrative as academic storytelling: A Chicano's search for presence and voice in academe. *International Journal of Qualitative Studies in Education, 18*(2), 147–163.

Alan, J. (2001, March). Hegel and black history. *Theory/Practice news and letters.* Retrieved August 5, 2004 from http://www.newsandletters.org/Issues/2001/March/1.03_brv.htm

Alexander-Smith, A. (2004). Feeling the rhythm of the critically conscious mind. *English Journal, 93*(3), 58–63.

Alim, H. S. (2005). Critical language awareness in the United States: Revisiting issues and revising pedagogies in a resegregated society. *Educational Researcher, 34*, 24–31.

Allen, P. G. (1986). *The sacred hoop: Recovering the feminine in American Indian tradition.* Boston: Beacon Press.

Alvermann, D. E., & Xu, S. H. (2003). Children's everyday literacies: Intersections of popular culture and language arts instruction. *Language Arts, 82*(2), 145–154.

Anzaldúa, G. (1990). *Borderlands, la frontera: The new mestiza.* San Francisco: Aunt Lute Books. (Original work published 1987)

Apple, M. (1982). *Education and power.* Boston: Routledge.

Apple, M. (1999). *Power, meaning, and identity: Essays in critical educational studies.* New York: Peter Lang.

Arthur, C. (Ed.). (1970). *Introduction. The German ideology: Part one* (pp. 4–34). New York: International Publishers.

Asher, N. (2005). At the interstices: Engaging postcolonial and feminist perspectives for a multicultural education pedagogy in the South. *Teachers College Record, 107*(5), 1079–1106.

Auerbach, E. (1991). Literacy and ideology. In W. Grabe (Ed.), *Annual review of applied linguistics* (pp. 71–85). New York: Cambridge University Press.

Auerbach, S. (2002). "Why do they give the good classes to some and not to others?" Latino parent narratives of struggle in a college access program. *Teachers College Record, 104*(7), 1369–1392.

Aveling, N. (2001). "Where do you come from?" Critical storytelling as a teaching strategy within the context of teacher education. *Discourse: Studies in the Cultural Politics of Education, 22*(1), 35–48.

Bacchi, C. (2000). Policy as discourse: What does it mean? Where does it get us? *Discourse: Studies in the Cultural Politics of Education, 21*(1), 45–57.

Ball, J. (2004). As if Indigenous knowledge and communities mattered. *American Indian Quarterly, 28*(3/4), 454–479.

Bambara, T. C. (Ed.). (1970). *The Black woman: An anthology.* New York: Signet.

Baquedano-Lopez, P. (2004). Traversing the center: The politics of language use in a Catholic religious education program. *Anthropology and Education Quarterly, 35*(2), 212–232.

Barnhart, R., & Kawagley, A. O. (2005). Indigenous knowledge systems and Alaskan Native ways of knowing. *Anthropology and Education Quarterly, 36*(1), 8–23.

Beck, A. S. (2005). A place for critical literacy. *Journal of Adolescent & Adult Literacy, 48*(5), 392–400.

Behar, R. (2001). Yellow marigolds for Ochún: An experiment in feminist ethnographic fiction. *International Journal of Qualitative Studies in Education, 14*(2), 107–116.

Berhoff, A. E. (1987). Foreword. In P. Freire & D. Macedo, *Literacy: Reading the word and the world* (pp. xi–xxiii). Westport, CT: Bergin & Garvey.

Best, S. (1995). *The politics of historical vision.* New York: Guilford Press.

Bishop, R. (2005). Freeing ourselves from neocolonial domination in research: A Kaupapa Maori approach to creating knowledge. In N. Denzin & Y. Lincoln (Eds.), *The Sage handbook of qualitative research* (3rd ed., pp. 109–138). Thousand Oaks, CA: Sage.

Blackburn, M. (2003). Exploring literacy performances and power dynamics at The Loft: Queer youth reading the world and the word. *Research in the Teaching of English, 37*(4), 467–490.

Blackburn, M. V. (2005). Agency in borderland discourses: Examining language use in a community center with Black queer youth. *Teachers College Record, 107*(1), 89–113.

Blair, H. A. (2000). Genderlects: Girl talk and boy talk in a middle-years classroom. *Language Arts, 77*(4), 315–323.

Bloome, D., & Carter, S. (2005). *Critical discourse analysis in and across educational contexts.* A workshop presented at the annual conference of National Council of Teachers of English Midwinter Assembly for Research. Columbus, OH, February 2005.

Bolin, R. (1968). *Immanuel Kant 's physical geography* (Trans. R. Boldin). Bloomington: Indiana University. (Original work published 1802)

Brandt, D. (2003). Changing literacy. *Teachers College Record, 105*(2), 245–260.

Brayboy, B. M. (2000). The Indian and the researcher: Tales from the field. *International Journal of Qualitative Studies in Education, 13*(4), 415–426.

Brodkey, L. (1987). Writing critical ethnographic narratives. *Anthropology & Education Quarterly, 18*(2), 67–76.

Bronner, S. (2002). *Of critical theory and its theorists* (2nd ed.). New York: Routledge.

Brookfield, S. (2003). Racializing the discourse of adult education. *Harvard Educational Review, 73*(4), 497–523.

Buck-Morss, S. (2000). Hegel and Haiti. *Critical Inquiry, 26*(4), 821–866.

Burns, L., & Morrell, E. (2005). Why critical discourse analysis in literacy research? *National Reading Conference Yearbook, 54*, 132–143.

Cahnmann, M. (2005). Translating competence in a critical bilingual classroom. *Anthropology and Education Quarterly, 36*(3), 230–249.

Carlson, D. (2001). Gay, queer, and cyborg: The performance of identity in a transglobal age. *Discourse: Studies in the Cultural Politics of Education, 22*(3), 297–309.

Carspecken, P. (1996). *Critical ethnography in educational research: A theoretical and practical guide.* New York: Routledge.

Carspecken, P., & Apple, M. (1992). Critical qualitative research: Theory, methodology, and practice. In M. LeCompte, W. Millroy, & J. Preissle (Eds.), *The handbook of qualitative research in education* (pp. 507–553). San Diego: Academic Press.

Case, R. E., Ndura, E., & Righettini, M. (2005). Balancing linguistic and social needs: Evaluating texts using a critical language awareness approach. *Journal of Adolescent and Adult Literacy, 48*(5), 374–391.

Chase, S. E. (2005). Narrative inquiry: Multiple lenses, approaches, and voices. In. N. Denzin & Y. Lincoln (Eds.), *The Sage handbook of qualitative research* (3rd ed., pp. 651–679). Thousand Oaks, CA: Sage.

Ching, S. D. (2005). Multicultural children's literature as an instrument of power. *Language Arts, 83*(2), 128–136.

Coffey, A., & Delamont, S. (2000). *Feminism and the classroom teacher: Research, praxis, and pedagogy.* New York: Routledge.

Collins, P. H. (1990). *Black feminist thought: Knowledge, consciousness, and the politics of empowerment.* New York: Routledge.

Collins, P. H. (1998). *Fighting words: Black women and the search for justice.* Minneapolis: University of Minnesota Press.

Collins, P. H. (2000). *Black feminist thought: Knowledge, consciousness, and the politics of empowerment* (2nd ed.). New York: Routledge. (Original work published 1990)

Collins, P. H. (2003).Toward a new vision. In M. Kimmel & A. L. Ferber (Eds.), *Privilege: A reader* (pp. 331-49). Boulder, CO: Westview.

Cone, J. H. (1970). *A Black theology of liberation.* Philadelphia: J. P. Lippencott.

Connor, J. J. (2003). "The textbooks never said anything about . . ." Adolescents respond to *The Middle Passage: White Ships/Black Cargo*—The use of a picture book with adolescents enhances and evokes aesthetic responses. *Journal of Adolescent and Adult Literacy, 47*(3), 240–246.

Cooks, J. (2004). Writing for something: Essays, raps, and writing preferences. *English Journal, 94*(1), 72–75.

Cooper, A. (1892). *A voice from the South.* Xenia, OH: Aldine.

Cowlishaw, G. K., & Frankenberg, R. (1999). *Rednecks, eggheads, and blackfellas: A study of racial power and intimacy in Australia.* Ann Arbor: University of Michigan Press.

Crenshaw, K. (1997). Color blindness, history, and the law. In W. Lumiano (Ed.), *The house that race built* (pp. 280–288). New York: Pantheon.

Crenshaw, K., Gotanda, N., Peller, G., & Thomas, K. (Eds.). (1995). *Critical race theory: The key writings that informed the movement.* New York: The New Press.

Cruz, C. (2001). Toward an epistemology of a brown body. *International Journal of Qualitative Studies in Education, 14*(5), 657–669.

Damico, J. S. (2005). Evoking hearts and heads: Exploring issues of social justice through poetry. *Language Arts, 83*(2), 137–146.

Darder, A. (2002). *Reinventing Paulo Freire: A pedagogy of love*. New York: Westview.

Darder, A., & Torres, R. (2005). *After race: Racism after multiculturalism*. New York: New York University Press.

Darder, A., Torres, R., & Gutiérrez, H. (Eds.). (1997). *Latinos and education: A critical reader*. New York: Routledge.

Davis, A., & James, J. (1998). *The Angela Davis reader*. Malden, MA: Blackwell.

DeBlase, G. (2003a). Acknowledging agency while accommodating romance: Girls negotiating meaning in literacy transactions. *Journal of Adolescent and Adult Literacy, 46*(8), 824–835.

DeBlase, G. L. (2003b). Missing stories, missing lives: Urban girls (re)constructing race and gender in the literacy classroom. *Urban Education, 38*(3), 270–329.

Delgado, R. (1984). The imperial scholar: Reflections on a review of civil rights literature. *University of Pennsylvania Law Review, 132*(3), 561–578.

Delgado, R. (Ed.). (1995). *Critical race theory: The cutting edge*. Philadelphia: Temple University Press.

Delgado, R., & Stefancic, J. (1997). *Critical white studies: Looking behind the mirror*. Philadelphia: Temple University Press.

Delgado, R., & Stefancic, J. (Eds.). (2000). *Critical race theory: The cutting edge* (2nd ed). Philadelphia: Temple University Press

Delgado, R., & Stefancic, J. (2001). *Critical race theory: An introduction*. New York: New York University Press.

Delgado Bernal, D. (1998). Using a Chicana feminist epistemology in educational research. *Harvard Educational Review, 68*(4), 555–582.

Delgado Bernal, D. (2001). Learning and living pedagogies of the home: The *mestiza* consciousness of Chicana studies. *International Journal of Qualitative Studies in Education,14*(5), 623–639.

Delgado Bernal, D. (2002). Critical race theory, Latino critical theory, and critical race-gendered epistemologies: Recognizing students of color as holders and creators of knowledge. *Qualitative Inquiry, 8*(1), 105–126.

Delgado-Gaitan, C. (1990). *Literacy for empowerment: The role of parents in children's education*. London: Falmer.

Delgado-Gaitan, C. (2005). Reflections from the field: Family narratives in multiple literacies. *Anthropology and Education Quarterly, 36*(3), 265–272.

Deloria, V. Jr. (1970). *We talk you listen: New tribes, new turf*. New York: Macmillan.

Deloria, V. Jr. (1983). Circling the same old rock. In W. Churchill (Ed.), *Marxism and Native Americans* (pp. 113–136). Boston: South End Press.

Deloria, V. Jr. (1994). *God is red: A native view of religion*. Golden, CO: Fulcrum.

Delpit, L. (2002). Introduction. In L. Delpit & J. Dowdy (Eds.), *The skin that we speak: Thoughts on language and culture in the classroom* (pp. xiii–xxiv). New York: The World Press.

Dillard, C. B. (2000). The substance of things hoped for, the evidence of things not seen: Examining an endarkened feminist epistemology in educational research and leadership. *International Journal of Qualitative Studies in Education, 13*(6), 661–681.

Dimitriadis, G. (2001). "In the clique": Popular culture, constructions of place, and the everyday lives of urban youth. *Anthropology and Education Quarterly, 32*(1), 29–51.

Douglass, F. (1886) *Three addresses on the relations subsisting between the White and Colored people of the United States*. Washington, DC: Gibson Bros.

Douglass, F. (1968). *Narrative of the life of Frederick Douglass, an American slave, written by himself.* New York: Signet. (Original work published 1882)

Dowdy, J. (2002). Ovuy Dyuh. In L. Delpit & J. Dowdy (Eds.), *The skin that we speak: Thoughts on language and culture in the classroom* (pp. 3–13). New York: The World Press.

Du Bois, W.E.B. (1899). *The Philadelphia Negro.* Boston, MA: Ginn and Co.

Du Bois, W.E.B. (1933). Marxism and the Negro Problem. *Crisis, 40*(5), 103–104, 118.

Du Bois, W.E.B. (1995). *The souls of black folk.* New York: Ginn and Co. (Original work published 1903)

Duncan, G. (2002a). Beyond love: A critical race ethnography of the schooling of adolescent Black males. *Equity and Excellence in Education, 35*(2), 131–143.

Duncan, G. (2002b). Critical race theory and method: Rendering race in urban ethnographic research. *Qualitative Inquiry, 8*(1), 85–104.

Duncan, G. A. (2005). Critical race ethnography in education: Narrative, inequality and the problem of epistemology. *Race, Ethnicity, and Education, 8*(1), 93–114.

Dryer, R. (1997). *White.* New York: Routledge.

Dyson, A. H. (1993). *Social worlds of children learning to write in an urban primary school.* New York: Teachers College Press.

Dyson, A. H. (2003a). Popular literacies and the "all" children: Rethinking literacy development for contemporary childhoods. *Language Arts, 81*(2), 100–109.

Dyson, A. H. (2003b). "Welcome to the Jam": Popular culture, school literacy, and the making of childhoods. *Harvard Educational Review, 73*(3), 328–361.

Edmondson, J. (2002). Asking different questions: Critical analyses and reading research. *Reading Research Quarterly, 37*(1), 113–119.

Elenes, C. A. (2001). Transformando fronteras: Chicana feminist transformative pedagogies. *International Journal of Qualitative Studies in Education, 14*(5), 689–702.

Elenes, C. A., Gonzalez, F. E., Bernal, D.D., & Villenas, S. (2001). Introduction: Chicana/Mexicana feminist pedagogies: *Consejos, respeto, y educación* in everyday life. *International Journal of Qualitative Studies in Education, 14*(5), 595–602.

Emberley, J. (1996). Aboriginal women's writing and the cultural politics of representation. *Women of the First Nations: Power, wisdom, and strength* (pp. 97–112). Winnipeg: University of Manitoba Press.

Eze, E. C. (1995). The color of reason: The idea of "race" in Kant's anthropology. In K. Faull (Ed.), *Anthropology and the German Enlightenment.* Lewisburg, PA: Bucknell University Press.

Eze, E. C. (Ed.). (1997). *Race and the enlightenment: A reader.* Cambridge, MA: Blackwell.

Fairclough, N. (1999). Global capitalism and critical awareness of language. *Language Awareness, 8*(2), 71–83.

Fairclough, N., & Wodak, R. (1997). Critical discourse analysis. In T. van Dijk (Ed.), *Discourse as social action* (pp. 258–284). London: Sage.

Fanon, F. (1965). *The wretched of the earth* (Trans. C. Farrington). New York: Grove Press. (original published 1961).

Fanon, F. (1967). *Black skin, white masks* (Trans. C. L. Markmann). New York: Grove Press. (Original published 1952)

Fay, B. (1987). *Critical social science: Liberation and its limits*. Ithaca, NY: Cornell University Press.

Feagin, J., & van Ausdale, D. (2001). *The first "R": How children learn race and racism*. New York: Rowman and Littlefield.

Fecho, B. (2000). Critical inquiries into language in an urban classroom. *Research in the Teaching of English, 34*(3), 368–395.

Fecho, B. (2001). "Why are you doing this?": Acknowledging and transcending threat in a critical literacy classroom. *Research in the Teaching of English, 36*(1), 9–37.

Fecho, B. (2002). Madaz publications: Polyphonic identity and existential literacy transactions. *Harvard Educational Review 72*(1), 93–119.

Ferber, A. L. (2007). Whiteness studies and the erasure of gender. *Sociology Compass, 1*(1), 265–282.

Fernández, L. (2002). Telling stories about school: Using critical race and Latino critical theories to document Latina/Latino education and resistance. *Qualitative Inquiry, 8*(1), 45–65.

Fernandez, N. (2001). The changing discourse on race in contemporary Cuba. *International Journal of Qualitative Studies in Education, 14*(2), 117–132.

Fine, M. (1991). *Framing dropouts: Notes on the politics of an urban high school*. Albany: State University of New York Press.

Fisher, M. (2003). Open mics and open minds: Spoken word poetry in African Diaspora participatory literacy communities. *Harvard Educational Review, 73*(3), 362–389.

Fisher, M. (2004). "The song is unfinished": The new literate and literary and their institutions. *Written Communication, 21*(3), 290–312.

Foley, D. E. (2001). Critical ethnography: The reflexive turn. *International Journal of Qualitative Studies in Education, 15*(5), 469–490.

Fordham, S. (1988). Racelessness as a factor in Black students' school success: Pragmatic strategy or pyrrhic victory? *Harvard Educational Review, 58*(1), 54–84.

Forgas, D. (Ed.). (2000). *The Antonio Gramsci reader: Selected writings 1916–1935*. New York: New York University Press.

Frankenberg, R. (1993). *White women, race matters: The social construction of whiteness*. Minneapolis: University of Minnesota Press.

Frankenberg, R., & Mani, L. (1993). Crosscurrents, crosstalk: Race, "postcoloniality" and the politics of location. *Cultural Studies, 7*(2), 292–310.

Freire, A., & Macedo, D., (Eds.). (1998). *The Paulo Freire Reader*. New York: Continuum.

Freire, P. (1970). *Pedagogy of the oppressed*. New York: Continuum.

Freire, P. (1971). Conscientisation—Unveiling and transforming reality. In C. Wright (Ed.), *Education for liberation and community* (pp. 3–6). Melbourne, Australia: Australian Council of Churches (revised from a talk given at Cuernavaca, Mexico).

Freire, P. (1987). The importance of the act of reading. In P. Freire & D. Macedo (Eds.), *Literacy: Reading the word and the world* (pp. 29–36). New York: Bergin and Garvey.

Freire, P. (1993). *Pedagogy of the city*. New York: Continuum.

Freire, P. (1995). *Pedagogy of hope: Reliving pedagogy of the oppressed*. New York: Continuum.

Freire, P. (1996). *Letters to Cristina: Reflections on my life and work* (Trans. D. Macedo, with Q. Macedo and A. Oliveria.). New York: Routledge.

Freire, P. (1998). *Teachers as cultural workers: Letters to those who dare teach.* Boulder, CO: Westview Press.

Freire, P. (2000). *Education for critical consciousness.* New York: Continuum. (Original work published in 1967)

Freire, P. (2002). *Education for critical consciousness.* New York: Continuum. (Original work published 1967, U.S. publication, 1973)

Freire, P., & Macedo, D. (1987). *Literacy: Reading the word and the world.* New York: Bergin and Garvey.

Gadotti, M. (1994). *Reading Paulo Freire: His life and work* (Trans. John Milton). Albany: State University of New York Press.

Gale, T. (2000). Putting academics in their place. *Australian Educational Researcher, 27*(2), 121–136.

Gallagher, C. (1995). "White reconstruction in the university." *Socialist Review, 24*(1/2), 165–87.

Galván, R. T. (2001). Portraits of Majors Desjuiciadas: Womanist pedagogies of the everyday, the mundane and the ordinary. *International Journal of Qualitative Studies in Education, 14*(5), 603–621.

Garcia, I. (1987). *Justice in Latin American theology of liberation.* Atlanta, GA: John Knox.

Gates, H. L. Jr. (1997). From the soul of suffering. Retrieved September 2, 2006, from http://www.pbs.org/newshour/gergan/march97/African_lit_3-7.html

Gayles, J. (2005). Playing the game and paying the price: Academic resilience among three high-achieving African American males. *Anthropology and Education Quarterly, 36*(3), 250–264.

Gilligan, C. (1982). *In a different voice.* Cambridge: Harvard University Press.

Gilyard, K. (2000). Literacy, identity, imagination, flight. *College Composition and Communication, 53*(2), 260–272.

Giroux, H. A. (1997). Rewriting the discourse of racial identity: Towards a pedagogy and politics of Whiteness. *Harvard Educational Review, 67*(2), 285–320.

Giroux, H. A. (1999). Critical pedagogy. Retrieved January 3, 2004, from http://www.perfectfit.org/CT/giroux2.html.

Gitlin, A., & Russell, R. (1994). Alternative methodologies and the research context. In A. Gitlin (Ed.), *Power and method: Political activism and educational research* (pp. 181–202). New York: Routledge.

Glazier, J., & Seo, J. (2005). Multicultural literature and discussion as mirror and window? *Journal of Adolescent & Adult Literacy, 48*(8), 686–700.

Gonick, M. (2003). *Between femininities: Ambivalence, identity, and the education of girls.* Albany: State University of New York Press.

González, F. E. (2001). *Haciendo que hacer*—cultivating a Mestiza worldview academic achievement: Braiding cultural knowledge into education research, policy, and practice. *International Journal of Qualitative Studies in Education, 14*(5), 641–656.

Gramsci, A. (1971). *Selections from the prison notebooks of Antonio Gramsci* (Ed. and Trans. Q. Hoare & G. Smith). New York: International Publishers.

Grande, S. (2000a). American Indian geographies of identity and power: At the crossroads of Indigena and Mestizaje. *Harvard Educational Review, 70*(4), 467–498.

Grande, S. (2000b). American identity and intellectualism: The quest for a red pedagogy. *International Qualitative Studies in Education, 13*(4), 343–359.

Grande, S. (2004). *Red pedagogy: Native American social and political thought.* New York: Rowman & Littlefield.

Graveline, F. J. (2000). Circle as methodology: Enacting an Aboriginal paradigm. *International Journal of Qualitative Studies in Education, 13*(4), 361–370.

Green, L. (2002). A descriptive study of African American English: Research in linguistics and education. *International Journal of Qualitative Studies in Education, 15*(6), 673–690.

Grossberg, L. (1994). Introduction: Bringin' it all back home—Pedagogy and cultural studies. In H. Giroux & P. McLaren (Eds.), *Between borders: Pedagogy and the politics of cultural studies* (pp. 1–28). New York: Routledge.

Guevara, E. (2003). *The motorcycle diaries: Notes on a Latin American journey.* Melbourne, Australia: Ocean Press.

Guzzetti, B. J., & Gamboa, M. (2004). Zines for social justice: Adolescent girls writing on their own. *Reading Research Quarterly, 39*(4), 408–436.

Guzzetti, B. J., & Gamboa, M. (2005). Online journaling: The informal writings of two adolescent girls. *Research in the Teaching of English, 40*(2), 168–206.

Gutiérrez, K. D. (2001). What's new in the English language arts: Challenging policies and practices, y qué? *Language Arts, 78*(6), 564–569.

Habermas, J. (1984). *The theory of communicative action.* Boston: Beacon Press.

Habermas, J. (1987). *Theory of communicative action,* Vols 1 & 2. Boston: Beacon Press. (Original work published 1981; republished 1984)

Haig-Brown, C. (2003). Creating spaces: Testimonio, impossible knowledge, and academe. *International Journal of Qualitative Studies in Education, 186* (3), 415–433.

Hall, S. (1970). Leisure, entertainment and mass communication. *Society and Leisure, 2,* 31, 170.

Hall, S. (1980). Encoding/decoding. In S. Hall, D. Hobson, A. Lowe, & P. Willis (Eds.), *Culture, media, language* (pp. 129–138). Birmingham, England: Centre for Contemporary Cultural Studies. (Original work published 1973)

Hall, S. (1982). The rediscovery of "ideology": Return of the repressed in media studies. In M. Gurevitch, T. Bennett, J. Curran, & J. Woollacott (Eds.), *Culture, society and the media* (pp. 56–90). London: Methuen.

Hall, S. (1984). Reconstruction work. *Ten 8, 16,* 1–10.

Hall, S. (1999). A conversation with Stuart Hall. *The Journal of the International Institute.* Retrieved April 9, 2005, from http://www.umich.edu/~iinet/journal/vol7no1/Hall.htm

Hall, S. (2000). Foreword. In D. A. Yon, *Elusive culture: Schooling, race, and identity in global times* (pp. ix–xii). Albany: State University New York Press.

Harrison, B., & Papa, R. (2005). The development of an Indigenous knowledge program in a New Zealand Maori-language immersion school. *Anthropology and Education Quarterly, 36*(1), 57–72.

Hefferman, L., & Lewison, M. (2005). What's lunch got to do with it? Critical literacy and discourse of the lunchroom. *Language Arts, 83*(2), 107–117.

Hegel, G. W. F. (1956). *The philosophy of history* (Trans. J. Sibree). New York: Dover.

Hegel, G. W. F. (1977). *The phenomenology of spirit* (Trans. A. V. Miller). Oxford: Oxford University Press. (Original work published 1807)

Hermes, M. (2005). "Ma'iingan is just a misspelling of the word wolf": A case for teaching culture through language. *Anthropology and Education Quarterly, 36*(1), 43–56.

Hernández, A. (1997). *Pedagogy, democracy, and feminism: Rethinking the public sphere.* Albany: State University of New York Press.

Hernández-Avila, I. (1995). Relocations upon relocations: Home, language, and Native American women's writings. *American Indian Quarterly, 19*, 491-507.

Hicks, D. (2000). Back to Oz? Rethinking the literary in a critical study of reading. *Research in the Teaching of English, 39*(1), 63-84.

Hinchman, K., & Young, J. (2001). Speaking but not being heard: Two adolescents negotiate classroom talk about text. *Journal of Literacy Research, 33*(2), 243-269.

Hinchman, K., Payne-Bourcy, L., Thomas, H., & Olcott, K. (2002). Representing adolescents' literacies: Case studies of three white males. *Reading Research and Instruction, 41*(3), 229-246.

Honeyghan, G. (2000). Rhythm of the Caribbean: Connecting oral history and literacy. *Language Arts, 77*(5), 406-413.

hooks, b. (1984). *From margin to center.* Boston: South End Press.

hooks, b. (1989). *Talking back: Thinking feminist, thinking black.* Boston: South End Press.

hooks, b. (1994). T*eaching to transgress: Education as the practice of freedom.* New York: Routledge.

Horkheimer, M., & Adorno, T. W. (1947). *Dialectic of Enlightenment.* (Original work published 1944 as *Philosophical fragments*)

Horton, M., with Kohl, J. & Kohl, H. (1998). *The long haul: An autobiography.* New York: Teachers College Press.

Hoy, D. C. (1991). A history of consciousness. *History of the human sciences, 4*(2), 261-281.

Hutchings, K. (2003). *Hegel and feminist philosophy.* Cambridge, MA: Polity Press.

Ismail, S. M., & Cazden, C. (2005). Struggles of Indigenous education and self-determination: Culture, context, and collaboration. *Anthropology and Education Quarterly, 36*(1), 88-92.

Janks, H. (2005). Deconstruction and reconstruction: Diversity as a productive resource. *Discourse: Studies in the Cultural Politics of Education, 26*(1), 31-43.

Jay, M. (1996). *The dialectical imagination: A history of the Frankfurt School and the Institute of Social Research, 1923-1950.* Berkeley: University of California Press. (Original work published 1973)

Jensen, R. (2005). *The heart of whiteness: Confronting race, racism, and white privilege.* San Francisco: City Lights.

Jiménez, R., Smith, P., & Martinez-León, N. (2003). Freedom and form: The language and literacy practices of two Mexican schools. *Reading Research Quarterly, 38*(4), 488-508.

Judy, R. A. (1991). Kant and the Negro. *Surfaces, 1*(8), 4-70. Retrieved June 21, 2006, from philosophy.eserver.org/judy-kant.pdf

Kalman, J. (2000). Learning to write in the street. *International Journal of Qualitative Studies in Education, 13*(3), 187-203.

Kant, I. (1784). *An answer to the question: What is enlightenment?* Retrieved December 26, 2000, from http://www.english.upenn.edu/~mgamer/Etexts/kant.html

Kant, I. (1965a). *Observations on the feeling of the beautiful and sublime.* (Trans. John T. Goldthwait). Berkeley: University of California Press. (Original work published 1764)

Kant, I. (1965b). *Critique of pure reason* (Trans. N. K. Smith). New York: St. Martin's Press. (Original work published 1781, 2nd ed. published 1787)

Kaomea, J. (2005). Indigenous strides in the elementary curriculum: A cautionary Hawaiian example. *Anthropology and Education Quarterly, 36*(1), 24–42.

Kawakami, A. J., & Dudoit, W. (2000). Ua Ao Hawai'i/Hawai'i is enlightened: Ownership in a Hawaiian language immersion classroom. *Language Arts, 77*(5), 384–390.

Kellner, D., & Share, J. (2005). Critical media literacy: Core concepts, debates, organizations, and policy. *Discourse: Studies in the Cultural Politics of Education, 26*(3), 369–386.

Kincheloe, J. (1998). Critical research in science education. In B. Fraser & K. Tobin (Eds.), *International handbook of science education* (pp. 1191–1205). Boston: Kluwer.

Kincheloe, J. (2004). *Critical theory primer.* New York: Peter Lang.

Kincheloe, J., & McLaren, P. (1994). Rethinking critical theory and qualitative research. In N. Denzin & Y. Lincoln (Eds.), *Handbook of qualitative research* (pp. 138–157). Thousand Oaks, CA: Sage.

Kincheloe, J. S., & McLaren, P. (2005). Rethinking critical theory and qualitative research. In N. Denzin & Y. Lincoln (Eds.), *Handbook of qualitative research* (3rd ed., pp. 303–342). Thousand Oaks, CA: Sage.

Kincheloe, J., Steinberg, S., Rodriguez, N., & Chennault, R. (Eds). (1998). *White reign: Deploying Whiteness in America.* New York: St. Martin's Press.

King, J. (1992). Diaspora literacy and consciousness in the struggle against miseducation in the Black community. *The Journal of Negro Education, 61*(3), 317–340.

King, M. L. Jr. (1963). *Letter from Birmingham jail.* Retrieved March 21, 2008, from http://patriotpost.us/histdocs/BirmJail.html

Klevan, A. (2002). Fighting the TAAS: The shedding of stereotypes at a bilingual high school. *International Journal of Qualitative Studies in Education, 15*(1), 43–54.

Knight, M. G., Norton, N. E., Bentley, C., & Dixon, I. R. (2004). The power of Black and Latina/o counterstories: Urban families and college-going processes. *Anthropology and Education Quarterly, 35*(1), 99–120.

Krell, D. F. (2000). The bodies of Black folk: From Kant and Hegel to DuBois and Baldwin. *boundary 2, 27*(3), 103–134.

Ladson-Billings, G. (1997). I know why this doesn't feel empowering: A critical race analysis of critical pedagogy. In P. Freire (Ed.), *Mentoring the mentor: A critical dialogue with Paulo Freire* (pp. 127–142). New York: Peter Lang.

Ladson-Billings, G. (2000). Racialized discourses and ethnic epistemologies. In N. Denzin & Y. Lincoln (Eds.), *Handbook of qualitative research* (2nd ed., pp. 257–277). Thousand Oaks, CA: Sage.

Ladson-Billings, G., & Donner, J. (2005). The moral activist role of Critical Race Theory scholarship. In N. Denzin & Y. Lincoln (Eds.), *The Sage handbook of qualitative research* (3rd ed., pp. 279–302). Thousand Oaks, CA: Sage.

Lamphere, L. (1994). Expanding our notions of "Critical qualitative methodology": Bringing race, class, and gender into the discussion (response). In A. Gitlin (Ed.), *Power and method: Political activism and educational research* (pp. 217–224). New York: Routledge.

LATCRIT: Latina & Latino Critical Legal Theory, Inc. (2007). Retrieved February 28, 2007, from http://www.latcrit.org/.

Lawrence, C., Matsuda, M., Delgado, R., & Crenshaw, K. (1993). Introduction. In M. Matusda, C. Lawrence, R., Delgado, & K. Crenshaw (Eds.), *Words that wound: Critical race theory, assaultive speech, and the First Amendment* (pp. 1–16). New York: Westview.

Lawrence-Lightfoot, S. (1994). *I've known rivers: Lives of loss and liberation.* New York: Addison-Wesley.

Lee, C. (2003). Why we need to re-think race and ethnicity in educational research. *Educational Researcher, 32*(5) 3–5.

Lee, S. J. (2004). Commentaries: Up against Whiteness: Students of Color in our schools. *Anthropology and Education Quarterly, 35*(1), 121–125.

Lefcourt, Y. K. (2005). *Navigating knowledge between two landscapes: (Re)envisioning Native Hawaiian education through ho'ola.* Unpublished dissertation. University of Illinois at Urbana-Champaign, IL.

Lefcourt, Y. K. (2006). Personal communication. November 8, 2006.

Lei, J. L. (2003). (Un)Necessary toughness?: Those "loud Black girls" and those "quiet Asian boys." *Anthropology and Education Quarterly, 34*(2), 158–181.

Leistyna, P., Woodrum, A., & Sherblom, S. A. (Eds.). (1996). Glossary. In P. Leistyna, A. Woodrum, & S. A. Sherblom (Eds.), *Breaking free: The transformative power of critical pedagogy* (pp. 333–344). Cambridge, MA: Harvard Educational Review. Reprint Series No. 27.

Leland, C. H., Harste, J. C., with Huber, K. R. (2005). Out of the box: Critical literacy in a first-grade classroom. *Language Arts, 82*(5), 257–268.

Lewis, C., & Fabos, B. (2005). Instant messaging, literacies, and social identities. *Reading Research Quarterly, 40*(4), 470–501.

Lewis, C., Ketter, J., & Fabos, B. (2001). Reading race in a cultural context. *International Journal of Qualitative Studies in Education, 14*(3), 317–350.

Li, G. (2003). Literacy, culture, and the politics of schooling: Counternarratives of a Chinese Canadian family. *Anthropology and Education Quarterly, 34*(2), 182–204.

Linné, R. (2003). Alternative textualities: Media culture and the proto-queer. *International Journal of Qualitative Studies in Education, 16*(5), 669–689.

Littlejohn, A., & Hicks, D. (2006). *Cambridge English Worldwide.* Cambridge: Cambridge University Press.

Lomawaima, K. T., & McCarty, T. L. (2002). When tribal sovereignty challenges democracy: American Indian education and the democratic ideal. *American Educational Research Journal, 39*(2), 279–305.

Lopez, N. (2002). Rewriting race and gender high school lessons: Second-generation Dominicans in New York City. *Teachers College Record, 104*(6), 1187–1203.

Lucey, H., & Reay, D. (2002). A market in waste: Psychic and structural dimensions of school-choice policy in the UK and children's narratives on "demonized" schools. *Discourse: Studies in the Cultural Politics of Education, 23*(3), 253–266.

Luke, A. (2004). Teaching after the market: From commodity to cosmopolitan. *Teachers College Record, 106*(7), 1422–1423.

Luke, A., & Freebody, P. (1997). Shaping the social practices of reading. In S. Muspratt, A. Luke, & P. Freebody (Eds.), *Constructing critical literacies* (pp. 185–225). Cresskill, NJ: Hampton.

Luke, C., & Gore, J. (Eds.). (1992). *Feminisms and critical pedagogy.* New York: Routledge.

Lyra, C. (1996). *As quarenta horas de Angicos: una experiência pioneira de educação*. São Paulo, Brazil: Cortez Editora.

Madison, D. S. (2005). *Critical ethnography: Method, ethics, and performance.* Thousand Oaks, CA: Sage.

Majors, Y. I.. (2004). "I wasn't scared of them, they were scared of me": Constructions of self/other in a Midwestern hair salon. *Anthropology and Education Quarterly, 35*(2), 167–188.

Manuelito, K. (2005). The role of education in American Indian self-determination: Lessons from the Ramah Navajo Community School. *Anthropology and Education Quarterly, 36*(1), 73–87.

Marcuse, H. (1968). *Negations: Essays in critical theory.* Boston: Beacon.

Marcuse, H. (1973). *Reason and revolution: Hegel and the rise of social theory.* London: Routledge and Kegan Paul. (Original work published 1941)

Marcuse, H. (1989). *Hegel's ontology and the theory of historicity/Herbert Marcuse* (Trans. S. Benhabib). Cambridge, MA: MIT Press.

Marker, M. (2000). Lummi identity and white racism: When location is a real place. *International Journal of Qualitative Studies in Education, 13*(4), 401–414.

Martinez-Roldan, C. M. (2003). Building worlds and identities: A case study of the role of narratives in bilingual literature discussions. *Research in Teaching of English, 37*(4), 491–526.

Marx, K. (1906). *Capital: A critique of political economy, Vol. I: The process of capitalist production* (Trans. S. and E. Aveling, from the Third German Edition of *Das Kapital;* Ed. F. Engels). Chicago: Charles H. Kerr and Co. (Original work published 1867)

Marx, K. (1977). Preface to a critique of political economy. In D. McLellan (Ed.), *Karl Marx: Selected writings* (pp. 388–392). Oxford, England: Oxford University.

Marx, K. (1996). *Das Kapital: A critique of political economy* (Ed., S. L. Levitsky). Washington, DC : Regnery.

Marx, K., & Engels, F. (1947). *The German ideology, parts I and II* (Ed., R. Pascal). New York: International Publishers.

Marx, K., & Engels, F. (1980). *The holy family: Or, critique of critical criticism.* Moscow: Foreign Languages Publishing House. (Original work published 1845)

Matthews, J. (2005). Visual culture and critical pedagogy in "Terrorist Times." *Discourse: Studies in the Cultural Politics of Education, 26*(2), 203–224.

McCarthy, T. (1978). *The critical theory of Jürgen Habermas.* Cambridge, MA: MIT Press.

McCarty, T. L., Borgoiakova, T., Gilmore, P., Lomawaima, K. T., & Romero, M. E. (Eds.). (2005). Editors' introduction: Indigenous epistemologies and education, self-determination, anthropology, and human rights. *Anthropology & Education Quarterly 36*(1), 1–7.

McIntyre, A. (1997). *Making meaning of whiteness: Exploring racial identity with white teachers.* Albany: State University of New York Press.

McLaren, P. (2004). [Faculty page]. Retrieved: February, 2006, from http://www.gseis.ucla. edu/faculty/pages/mclaren

McLaren, P., & Giarelli, J. (Eds.). (1995). *Critical theory and educational research.* Albany: State University of New York Press.

Meadmore, D., & Meadmore, P. (2004). The boundlessness of performativity in elite Australian schools. *Discourse: Studies in the Cultural Politics of Education, 25*(3), 375–387.

Meador, E. (2005). The making of marginality: Schooling for Mexican immigrant girls in the rural Southwest. *Anthropology and Education Quarterly, 36*(2), 149–164.

Medina, C. (2004). Drama wor(l)ds: Explorations of Latina/o realistic fiction through drama. *Language Arts, 81*(4), 272–282.

Merchant, G. (2001). Teenagers in cyberspace: Language use and language change in Internet chatrooms. *Journal of Research in Reading, 24*(3), 293–306.

Merchant, G. (2005). Electronic involvement: Identity performance in children's informal digital writing. *Discourse: Studies in the Cultural Politics of Education, 26*(3), 301–314.

Meyer, M. (2000). Between theory, method, and politics: Positioning of the approaches to CDA. In R. Wodak & M. Meyer (Eds.), *Methods of critical discourse analysis* (pp. 14–31). London: Sage.

Michaels, W. B. (2006). *The trouble with diversity: How we learned to love identity and ignore inequality.* New York: Metropolitan Books.

Moje, E. B. (2000). "To be part of the story": The literacy practices of gansta adolescents. *Teachers College Record, 102*(3), 651–690.

Moje, E. B., Ciechanowski, K. M., Kramer, K., Ellis, L., Carrillo, R., & Collazo, T. (2004). Working toward third space in content area literacy: An examination of everyday funds of knowledge and discourse. *Reading Research Quarterly, 39*(1), 38–70.

Moll, L. C., Armanti, C., Neff, D., & Gonzalez, N. (1992). Funds of knowledge for teaching: Using a qualitative approach to connect homes and classrooms. *Theory into Practice, 31*(2), 132–141.

Möller, K., & Allen, J. (2000). Connecting, resisting, and searching for safer places: Students respond to Mildred Taylor's *The Friendship. Journal of Literacy Research, 32*(2), 145–186.

Monahan, M. B. (2003). "On the lookout for language": Children as language detectives. *Language Arts, 80*(3), 206–214.

Monzó, L. D., & Rueda, R. (2003). Shaping education through diverse funds of knowledge: A look at one Latina paraeducator's lived experiences, beliefs, and teaching practice. *Anthropology and Education Quarterly, 34*(1), 72–95.

Morrell, E. (2002). Toward a critical pedagogy of popular culture: Literacy development among urban youth. *Journal of Adolescent and Adult Literacy, 46*(1), 72–77.

Morrell, E. (2004a). *Linking literacy and popular culture: Finding connections for lifelong learning.* Norwood, MA: Christopher-Gordon.

Morrell, E. (2004b). *Becoming critical researchers: Literacy and empowerment for urban youth.* New York: Peter Lang.

Morrell, E. (2005). Critical English education. *English Education, 37*(4), 312–321.

Morrell, E., & Collatos, A. M. (2002). Toward critical teacher education: High school students sociologist as teacher educators. *Social Justice, 29*(4), 60–70.

Morrell, E., & Duncan-Andrade, J. (2002). Promoting academic literacy with urban youth through engaging in hip-hop culture. *English Journal, 91*(6), 88–92.

Morrell, E., & Duncan-Andrade, J. (2004). What youth do learn in school: Using hip-hop as a bridge to canonical poetry. In J. Mahiri (Ed.), *What they don't learn in school: Literacy in the lives of urban youth* (pp. 247–268). New York: Peter Lang.

Morrison, T. (1992). *Playing in the dark: Whiteness and the literary imagination.* Cambridge, MA: Harvard University Press.

Nicholson, L. J. (1986). *Gender and history: The limits of social theory in the age of the family*. New York: Columbia University Press.

Oliver, M., & Shapiro, T. (1995). *Black wealth/White wealth: A new perspective on racial inequality*. New York: Routledge.

Olivo, W. (2003). "Quit talking and learn English!" Conflicting language ideologies in an ESL classroom. *Anthropology and Education, 34*(1), 50–71.

Olivio, W., & de Valladolid, C. E. (2005). *Entre la Espada y la Pared*: Critical educators, bilingual education, and educational reform. *Journal of Latinos and Education, 4*(4), 283–293.

Omolade, B. (1993). A Black feminist pedagogy. *Women's Studies Quarterly, 15*(3/4), 32–39.

Orellana, M. F. (2001). The work kids do: Mexican and Central American immigrant children's contributions to households and schools in California. *Harvard Educational Review, 71*(3), 366–389.

Otoya-Knapp, K. (2004). When Central City High School students speak: Doing critical inquiry for democracy. *Urban Education, 39*(2), 149–171.

Pecora, V. & Irr, C. (2005). The Frankfurt School. In M. Groden, M. Kreisworth, & I. Szeman (Eds.), *Johns Hopkins guide to literary theory and criticism* (3rd ed., pp. 361-365). Baltimore, MD: Johns Hopkins University Press.

Pennycook, A., & Coutand-Marin, S. (2003). Teaching English as a missionary language. *Discourse: Studies in the Cultural Politics of Education, 24*(3), 337–353.

Pilcher, J. K. (2001). Engaging to transform: Hearing Black women's voices. *International Journal of Qualitative Studies in Education, 14*(3), 283–303.

Pizarro, M. (1998). "Chicana/o power!" Epistemology and methodology for social justice and empowerment in Chicana/o communities. *Qualitative Studies in Education, 11*(1), 57–80.

Popkewitz, T., & Fendler, L. (Eds.). (1999). *Critical theories in education: Changing terrains of knowledge and politics*. New York: Routledge.

Pratt, M. (1991). Arts of the contact zone. *Profession, 91*, 33–40.

Prendergast, C. (2002). The economy of literacy: How the Supreme Court stalled the civil rights movement. *Harvard Educational Review, 72*(2), 206–229.

Quantz, R. (1992). On critical ethnography (with some postmodern considerations). In M. LeCompte, W. Millroy, & J. Preissle (Eds.), *The handbook of qualitative research in education* (pp. 447–505). San Diego: Academic Press.

Quiroz, P. A. (2001). The silencing of Latino student "voice": Puerto Rican and Mexican narratives in eighth grade and high school. *Anthropology and Education Quarterly, 32*(3), 326–349.

Reed, G. G. (2003). Fastening and unfastening identities: Negotiating identity in Hawai'i. *Discourse: Studies in the Cultural Politics of Education, 22*(3), 327–339.

Re'em, M. (2001). The politics of normalcy: Intersectionality and the construction of difference in Christian–Jewish relations. *International Journal of Qualitative Studies in Education, 14*(3), 381–397.

Rodriguez, N. (2000). Projects of Whiteness in a critical pedagogy. In N. Rodriguez & L. Villaverde (Eds.), *Dismantling White privilege: Pedagogy, politics, and Whiteness* (pp. 1–24). New York: Peter Lang.

Roediger, D. R. (2001). Critical studies of Whiteness, USA: Origins and Arguments. *Theoria*, 72–97.

Rogers, R. L. (2000). "It's not really writing, it's just answering the questions." *Language Arts, 77*(5), 428–437.

Rogers, R. (2002a). Through the eyes of the institution: A critical discourse analysis of decision making in two special education meetings. *Anthropology and Education Quarterly, 33*(2), 213–237.

Rogers, R. (2002b). "That's what your're here for, you're suppose to tell us": Teaching and learning critical literacy. *Journal of Adolescent and Adult Literacy, 45*(8), 772–787.

Rogers, R. (2002c). Between contexts: A critical discourse analysis of family literacy, discursive practices, and literate subjectivities. *Reading Research Quarterly, 37*(3), 248–277.

Rogers, R. (2004). Storied selves: A critical discourse analysis of adult learners' literate lives. *Reading Research Quarterly, 39*(3), 272–305.

Rogers, R., Kramer, M. A., Mosley, M., Fuller, C., Light, R., Nehart, M., Jones, R., Beaman-Jones, S., DePasquale, J., Hobson, S., & Thomas, P. (2005). Professional development as social transformation: The literacy for social justice teacher research group. *Language Arts, 82*(5), 347–358.

Rogers, T., Tyson, C., & Marshall, E. (2000). Living dialogues in one neighborhood: Moving toward understanding across discourses and practices of literacy and schooling. *Journal of Literacy Research, 32*(1), 1–12.

Romero, M. E. (2002). Nurturing and validating Indigenous epistemologies in higher education: Comment on "Domestication of the Ivory Tower." *Anthropology & Education Quarterly, 33*(2),250–254.

Rumberger, R. W., & Gándara, P. (2004). Seeking equity in the education of California's English language learners. *Teachers College Record, 106*(10), 2032–2056.

Rymes, B., & Anderson, K. (2004). Second language acquisition for all: Understanding the interactional dynamics of classrooms in which Spanish and AAE are spoken. *Research in the Teaching of English, 39*(2), 107–135.

Sandoval, C. (1998). *Mestizaje* as method: Feminists of color challenge the canon. In C. Trujillo (Ed.), *Living Chicana theory* (pp. 352–370). Berkeley: Third Woman Press.

Sandoval, C. (2000). *Methodology of the oppressed.* Minneapolis: University of Minnesota Press.

Sarte, J. (1968). Preface. In F. Fanon, *Wretched of the Earth.* New York: Grove Press.

Schott, R. (Ed.). (1997). *Feminist interpretations of Immanuel Kant.* College Park: Pennsylvania State University Press.

Selfa, L. (2002). Slavery and the origins of racism. *International Socialist Review, 26.* Retrieved April 19, 2006, from http://www.isreview.org/issues/26/roots_of_racism.shtml

Shannon. P. (2000). "What's my name?" A politics of literacy in the latter half of the 20th century in America. *Reading Research Quarterly, 35*(1), 90–107.

Shaw, K. (2004). Using feminist critical policy analysis in the realm of higher education: The case of welfare reform as gendered educational policy. *The Journal of Higher Education, 75*(1), 56–79.

Sheehy, M. (2002). Illuminating constructivism: Structure, discourse, and subjectivity in a middle school classroom. *Reading Research Quarterly, 37*(3), 278–309.

Sherman, H. (1976). Dialectics as a method. *Critical Sociology, 6*(4), 57–64.

Shor, I. (1980). *Critical teaching and everyday life.* Chicago: University of Chicago Press

Shor, I. (1987). *Freire for the classroom: A sourcebook for liberatory teaching.* Portsmouth, NH: Boynton/Cook Publishers.

Shor, I. (1999). What is critical literacy? *Journal of Pedagogy, Pluralism, & Practice, 4*(1), 1–21.

Silko, L. M. (1996). *Yellow woman and a beauty of the spirit: Essays on Native American life today.* New York: Simon & Schuster.

Sleeter, C. (1996). *Multicultural education as social activism.* Albany: State University of New York Press.

Smith, L. T. (1999). *Decolonizing methodologies: Research and Indigenous peoples.* London: Zed Books.

Smith, L. T. (2005). Building a research agenda for Indigenous epistemologies and education. *Anthropology and Education Quarterly, 36*(1), 93–95.

Solórzano, D. G., Ceja, M., & Yosso, T. (2000). Critical race theory, racial microagressions, and campus racial climate: The experiences of African American college students. *The Journal of Negro Education, 69*(1/2), 60–73.

Solórzano, D. G., & Delgado Bernal, D. (2001). Examining transformational resistance through a critical race and LatCrit theory framework: Chicana and Chicano students in an urban context. *Urban Education, 36*(3), 308–342.

Solórzano, D., & Yosso, T. (2001). Critical race and LatCrit theory: Counterstorytelling: The Chicana and Chicano graduate school experience. *International Journal of Qualitative Studies in Education, 14*(4), 471–495.

Solórzano, D., & Yosso, T. (2002). Critical race methodology: Counterstorytelling as an analytic framework for education research. *Qualitative Inquiry, 8*(1), 23–44.

Solsken, J., Willett, J., & Wilson-Keenan, J. (2000). Cultivating hybrid texts in multicultural classrooms: Promise and challenge. *Research in the Teaching of English, 35*(2), 179–212.

Stafford, A. M. (1997). The feminist critique of Hegel on women and the family. *Animus, 2.* Retrieved April 18, 2006, from http://www.mun.ca/animus/1997vol2/staford1.htm

Stovall, D. O. (2005). A challenge to traditional theory: Critical race theory, African American community organizers, and education. *Studies in the Cultural Politics of Education, 26*(1), 95–108.

Suina, J. H. (2004). Native language teachers in a struggle for language and cultural survival. *Anthropology and Education Quarterly, 35*(3), 281–302.

Sumida, A. Y. (2000). Reading a child's writing as a social text. *Language Arts, 77*(4), 309–314.

Sutherland, L. M. (2005). Black adolescent girls' use of literacy practices to negotiate boundaries of ascribed identity. *Journal of Literacy Research, 37*(3), 365–406.

Sydie, R. A. (1987). *Natural women cultured men: A feminist perspective on sociological theory.* Toronto: Methuen.

Tate, W. (1997). Critical race theory and education: History, theory, and implications. *Review of Research in Education, 22*(1), 195–247.

Taxel, J. (2002). Children's literature at the turn of the century: Toward a political economy of the publishing industry. *Research in the Teaching of English, 37*(2) 145–197.

Taylor, M. D. (1987). *The friendship.* New York: Dial.

Tejeda, C. (2005). *Toward a literacy of the spaces of learning: Reading and writing the spaces of literacy development in neocolonial contexts and classrooms.* National Council of Teachers of English Assembly for Research, Mid-winter Conference February, Columbus, OH, February, 2005.

Thompson, A. (2003). Tiffany, friend of people of Color: White investments in antiracism. *International Journal of Qualitative Studies in Education, 65*(1), 7–29.

Thompson, J. (1984). *Studies in the theory of ideology*. Cambridge, UK: Polity Press.

Thompson, J. B. (1990). *Ideology and modern culture*. Cambridge, UK: Polity Press.

Trainor, J. S. (2005). "My ancestors didn't own slaves:" Understanding White talk about race. *Research in the Teaching of English, 40*(2), 140–167.

Traueb, E. T. (1998). *Latinos Unidos: From cultural diversity to the politics of solidarity*. Lanham, MD: Rowman & Littlefield Publishers.

Traueb, E. T. (1999). Critical ethnography and a Vygotskian pedagogy of hope: The empowerment of Mexican immigrant children. *Qualitative Studies in education, 12*(6), 591–614.

Valle, V., & Torres, R. (1994). Latinos in a "post-industrial" disorder: Politics of a changing city. *Socialist Review, 23*(4), 1–28.

Valle, V., & Torres, R. (1995). The idea of *mestizaje* and the "race" problematic: Racialized media discourse in a post-Fordist landscape. In A. Darder (Ed.), *Culture and difference: Critical perspectives on the bi-cultural experience in the United States* (pp. 139–153). Westport, CT: Bergin & Garvey.

van Dijk, T. (1991). *Racism and the press*. London: Sage.

van Dijk, T. (1993). *Discourse and elite racism*. London: Sage.

Verharen, C. (1997). "The New World and the dreams to which it may give rise": An African and American response to Hegel's challenge. *Journal of Black Studies, 27*(4), 456–494.

Villenas, S. (1996). The colonizer/colonized Chicana ethnographer: Identity, marginalization, and co-optation in the field. *Harvard Education Review, 66*(4), 771–731.

Villenas, S. (2001). Latina mothers and small-town racisms: Creating narratives of dignity and moral education in North Carolina. *Anthropology and Education Quarterly, 32*(1), 3–28.

Villenas, S. (2005). Commentary. Latina literacies in *Convivencia*: Communal spaces of teaching and learning. *Anthropology and Education Quarterly, 36*(3), 273–277.

Walker, A. (1983). *In search of our mothers' gardens: Womanist prose*. San Diego: Harcourt Brace Jovanovich.

Walker, D. (1830). *Walker's appeal, in four articles; together with a preamble, to the coloured citizens of the world, but in particular, and very expressly, to those of the United States of America, written in Boston, state of Massachusetts, September 28, 1829*. Boston: Revised and Published by David Walker.

Walkerdine, V. (1990). *Schoolgirl fictions*. London: Verso.

Wallace, C. (1999). Critical language awareness: Key principles for a course in critical reading. *Multilingual Matters, 8*(2), 98–110. Retrieved August 23, 2007, from http://www.multilingual-matters.net/la/008/la0080098.htm

Weiler, K. (1991). Freire and a feminist pedagogy of difference. Harvard Educational Review, 61(4), 449–474.

Weis, L., & Fine, M. (2001). Extraordinary conversations in public schools. *International Journal of Qualitative Studies in Education, 14*(4), 497–523.

Weis, L., & Lombardo, S. L. (2003). Producing Whiteness: An exploration of working-class White men in two contexts. *Discourse: Studies in the Cultural Politics of Education, 23*(1), 5–25.

West, C. (1988). *Toward a socialist theory of racism*. Retrieved August 7, 2004, from http://www.eserver.org/race/toward-a-theory-of-racism.html.

West, C. (1993a). *Keeping faith: Philosophy and race in America*. New York: Routledge.

West, C. (1993b). The new politics of difference. In C. McCarthy & W. Crichlow (Eds.), *Race identity and representation in education* (pp. 11–23). New York: Routledge.

West, C. (1995). Foreword. In K. Crenshaw, N. Gotanda, G. Peller, & K. Thomas (Eds.), *Critical race theory: The key writings that formed the movement* (pp. xi-xii). New York: The New Press.

West, C. (2004). *Democracy matters: Winning the fight against imperialism*. New York: Penguin.

Wheeler, R. S., & Swords, R. (2004). Codeswitching: Tools of language and culture transform the dialectally diverse classroom. *Language Arts, 81*(6), 470–480.

Wiggershaus, R. (1994). *The Frankfurt School: Its history, theories, and political significance* (Trans. Michael Robertson). Cambridge, MA: The MIT Press.

Wiggershaus, R. (2006). *Learning from each other*. Retrieved, November 1, 2007, from http://www.goethe.de/wis/fut/dos/gdw/wig/en1786350.htm

Williams, S. O. (2006). T*he mis-education of the Negro continues: The connection between the beginning reading instruction delivered to three high performing Black girls and the instruction delivered within schools designed to colonize.* Unpublished dissertation. University of Illinois at Urbana–Champaign.

Willis, A. I. (1997). Historical considerations. *Language Arts, 74*(5), 387–397

Willis, A. I. (2005). *Beyond academic arrogance: Critically conscious literacy research and practice*. A response to Garrett A. Duncan at the annual meeting of the National Council of Teachers of English Assembly for Research, Columbus, OH, February 2005.

Wodak, R. (1996). *Disorders of discourse*. New York: Longman.

Woodson, C. G. (1933). *The mis-education of the Negro*. Washington, DC: Associated Publishers.

Woodson, C. G. (1942). *The story of the Negro retold* (3rd ed.). Washington, DC: The Associated Publishers, Inc.

Woodson, C. G., (Ed.). (1942b). *The works of Francis J. Grimke*. Washington, DC: Associated Publishers.

Wynne, J. (2002). "We don't talk right. You ask him." In L. Delpit & J. Dowdy (Eds.), *The skin that we speak: Thoughts on language and culture in the classroom* (pp. 203–219). New York: The World Press.

X, Malcolm. (1965). *The autobiography of Malcolm X*. (With the assistance of Alex Haley.) New York: Grove Press.

Yosso, T. J. (2005a). Whose culture has capital? A critical race theory discussion of community cultural wealth. *Race, Ethnicity, and Education, 8*(1), 69–91.

Yosso, T. J. (2005b). *Critical race counterstories along the Chicana/Chicano educational pipeline*. New York: Routledge.

Young, J. (2000). Boy talk: Critical literacy and masculinities. *Reading Research Quarterly, 35*(3), 312–337.

Young, J. (2001). Displaying practices of masculinity: Critical literacy and social contexts. *Journal of Adolescent and Adult Literacy, 45*(1), 4–14.

Index

About the Authors

Arlette Ingram Willis received her Ph. D. from the Ohio State University. She is currently a professor at the University of Illinois at Urbana-Champaign in the Department of Curriculum and Instruction, the division of Language and Literacy. Her publications include *Teaching and Using Multicultural Literature in Grades 9–12: Moving Beyond the Canon* (1998); *Reading Comprehension Research and Testing in the U.S.: Undercurrents of Race, Class, and Power in the Struggle for Meaning* (2008); *Multiple and Intersecting Identities in Qualitative Research* (co-edited with B. Merchant, 2001); *Multicultural Issues in Literacy Research and Practice* (co-edited with G. Garcia, R. Barrera, and V. Harris); and numerous articles, monographs, and book chapters.

LaTanya (Burke) Lambert is currently the lead teacher at Austin Polytechnic Academy (APA). LaTanya has been teaching in the Chicago Public School district for the past 8 years. She has extensive experience in the realm of small school development as a pioneer teacher at Small School of Entrepreneurship at South Shore campus and now as lead teacher and programmer at APA. She is currently pursuing an administrative certificate in an effort to help assist in the production of effective future urban educators.

Helena Hall received her Ph.D. from the Department of Curriculum and Instruction, the Language and Literacy division, at the University of Illinois at Urbana-Champaign. She also earned doctoral certificates in Writing Studies and in Second Language Acquisition and Teacher Education (SLATE). During her graduate career, she taught a variety of composition classes at the University of Illinois and worked at the University's Writing Center. Her major research interests are writing across the curriculum and second language literacy (second language writing development, assessment, and instruction). Currently, Helena is the Writing Center director at Loras College in Dubuque, Iowa.

Ana Lucia Herrera is a first-generation immigrant who lives and teaches elementary school in Chicago. She received her Bachelor's and Master's degrees from the University of Illinois. She has presented her research on language, literacy, and identity at national conferences. Currently, she enjoys the privilege of sharing her life with little people who teach her how to become a more compassionate, tolerant, and loving person.

Catherine Hunter is the Research Assistant for the Center for Education in Small Urban Communities. She is also a doctoral candidate in Curriculum and Instruction, the division of Language and Literacy. Ms. Hunter is a certified Teacher Support Specialist and has taught secondary English literature, reading, and French in Dougherty County, Albany, Georgia from 1990–1999. Her research interests are literacy education at the secondary level, specifically in the areas of socio-cultural influences on literacy and schooling, and the literacy education of culturally and linguistically diverse students. Her publications are: *Reflective writing: Transforming lives, ideas, and the future of English education* (2007, with A. Willis, in K. Keaton and S. Vavra (Eds.), *Closing the Gap: English Educators Address the Tensions Between Teacher Preparation and Teaching Writing in the Secondary Schools*; and a review of P. C. Murrell Jr.'s *African-Centered Pedagogy: Developing Schools of Success for African American Children* in the *Journal of Curriculum Studies, 35*(3), 39–403 (2003, with L. A. Buckley, J. J. Connor, and S. O. Williams).

Mary Veronica Montavon was born in Washington, D. C. She taught in private schools in Chicago and Guatemala City and in public schools in rural southern Illinois for 15 years. She coordinated and directed the Migrant Education and Bilingual Education programs in one rural district for more than a decade before receiving her Ph.D. from the University of Illinois in Urbana-Champaign in 2003. She is currently a lecturer in the Department of Linguistics at Southern Illinois University where she teaches endorsement courses for ESL and bilingual teachers in the MATESOL Program. Her scholarly interests include second language literacy, critical literacy, and sociocultural impediments to equitable education.